DESIGNING THE ONLINE LEARNING EXPERIENCE

DESIGNING THE ONLINE LEARNING EXPERIENCE

Evidence-Based Principles and Strategies

Simone C. O. Conceição and Les L. Howles

Foreword by B. Jean Mandernach

STERLING, VIRGINIA

COPYRIGHT © 2021 BY STYLUS PUBLISHING, LLC.

Published by Stylus Publishing, LLC.
22883 Quicksilver Drive
Sterling, Virginia 20166-2019

Library of Congress Cataloging-in-Publication Data
The CIP for this text has been applied for.

13-digit ISBN: 978-1-62036-834-3 (cloth)
13-digit ISBN: 978-1-62036-835-0 (paperback)
13-digit ISBN: 978-1-62036-836-7 (library networkable e-edition)
13-digit ISBN: 978-1-62036-837-4 (consumer e-edition)

Printed in the United States of America

All first editions printed on acid-free paper
that meets the American National Standards Institute
Z39-48 Standard.

Bulk Purchases

Quantity discounts are available for use in workshops and for staff development.

Call 1-800-232-0223

First Edition, 2021

This book is dedicated to instructors and learning designers who had to rethink and retool existing courses for the online environment during the COVID-19 pandemic.

CONTENTS

FOREWORD   ix
     B. Jean Mandernach

PREFACE   xiii

1   DESIGNING FOR THE LEARNER EXPERIENCE   1

2   INTEGRATED FRAMEWORK FOR DESIGNING THE ONLINE
    LEARNING EXPERIENCE   15

3   DESIGNING THE COURSE STRUCTURE AND LEARNER INTERFACE   39

4   FACILITATING LEARNING THROUGH INSTRUCTIONAL
    CONTENT DESIGN   61

5   CREATING MEANINGFUL LEARNING ACTIVITIES THROUGH
    LEARNING EXPERIENCE DESIGN   85

6   ENHANCING MOTIVATION, ENGAGEMENT, AND LEARNING
    THROUGH SOCIAL INTERACTIONS   103

7   INCORPORATING ASSESSMENTS AND FEEDBACK THROUGHOUT
    THE LEARNING EXPERIENCE   121

8   PUTTING IT TOGETHER   137

GLOSSARY   153

REFERENCES   161

ABOUT THE AUTHORS   175

INDEX   177

In higher education, it is unusual for a book to be published at exactly the right time to make an immediate and profound impact. Although a handful of books are visionary and published in advance of predicted challenges, the vast majority are written in response to current needs and, despite being informative, arrive on the market well beyond the optimal time to have the greatest influence. Regardless of whether a book is published a bit too early or a bit too late, the practical impact is often diminished as a sheer byproduct of timing.

Designing the Online Learning Experience is the rare exception. With over 50 combined years as distance education scholars, practitioners, and thought-leaders, Simone C.O. Conceição and Les L. Howles fully understand the ever-evolving nature of online education and anticipated the growing need for learning experience online design. Our conversations as colleagues on the *eLearn Magazine* editorial board centered around a growing unrest . . . a dissatisfaction with traditional approaches to instructional design. At the heart of our discussions was an awareness that our knowledge of online education and our experiences as online instructors were not enough. To do something meaningful—something actionable—we needed to shift our perspective to focus on those who matter most. The missing element in the available literature was a comprehensive approach to online course design that aligns research and experience with the needs, perceptions, and realities of those at the center of it all: students.

While I and most of my colleagues were content to stand around the virtual watercooler complaining about this disconnect, Conceição and Howles set out to fix it. Hence, the philosophy and ideas underlying *Designing the Online Learning Experience* were born.

Then the COVID-19 pandemic hit. Higher education—all higher education—was thrusted suddenly and unexpectedly into virtual teaching and learning. While the need for more holistic online course design was already an emerging issue, the COVID-19 pandemic catapulted concerns to the forefront. Online teaching and learning were no longer reserved exclusively for those who chose it. It impacted everyone. Questions skyrocketed. Concerns skyrocketed. Dissatisfaction with the status quo of online education skyrocketed.

Simply put, thanks to the pervasive, global immersion into online education, time for contemplation has run out. It is time for action. It is time for a fundamental shift in our philosophy of online teaching and our approach to online course design. Fortunately, *Designing the Online Learning Experience* arrives just in time to make this happen. With research-driven, practitioner-proven strategies, it is poised to make an immediate and profound impact on not only those new to online education but also experienced instructors seeking to create a more engaging online learning experience for their students.

There is a host of available literature addressing virtually every aspect of distance education. From assessment to technology (and everything in between), there are books, journals, websites, and podcasts dedicated exclusively to promoting best practices in online teaching. Admittedly, I am a frequent contributor—as a researcher, author, and journal editor—of these disparate best-practice findings. But despite this plethora of information, what was missing—until now—was an holistic approach to online course design that comprehensively addresses the cognitive, social, emotional, and behavioral aspects of the learning experience. It is not a matter of needing more information. Rather, the greatest need is for an actionable philosophy and framework that fosters effective design decisions using relevant research in concert with the learners' experiences.

Key to this endeavor is a focus on the *learners' experiences*. This is more than instructional design. Instructional design applies research principles to design, develop, and deliver online courses; it is necessary but not sufficient. Instructional design centers around the expertise and decisions of the content expert but fails to fully embrace learner empathy as a driving factor in course design. Recognizing the limitations of traditional approaches, theorists have offered a wide range of alternatives: learner-centered design, human-centered design, user-experience design, participatory design, emotional design, empathic design . . . the list goes on and on. Like traditional instructional design, these approaches are relevant and valuable. Like traditional instructional design, they are necessary but not sufficient. Or, perhaps more accurately, when viewed in combination, sufficient but disconnected. Learning experience design connects these philosophies to offer a holistic approach to online course design that transcends individual, independent design strategies. As explained by Conceição and Howles, "Learning experience design . . . require[s] a different mindset, process, and toolkit for instructors and course designers" (p. 13, this volume).

Designing the Online Learning Experience delivers the inspiration and guidance that online instructors and course designers need *right now*. While the COVID-19 pandemic will undoubtedly end, the widespread repercussions of higher education's immersion in online education will not.

Experienced online instructors were forced to dig deeper and think differently to meet student demands that had not previously existed. Instructors new to online teaching were pressed to reconsider the fundamental meaning of effective teaching and explore the potential available via online education. The questions, concerns, and challenges raised during the pandemic-induced shift to online teaching and learning are not likely to fade as we return to "normal." Higher education is ripe for a new approach to meaningful, engaging, learner-centered online education. And *Designing the Online Learning Experience* provides it.

B. Jean Mandernach, PhD
Research Professor and Executive Director
Center for Innovation in Research and Teaching
Grand Canyon University
September 2020

The number of students taking at least one distance education course from fall 2015 to fall 2016 accounted for 6,359,121 individuals (representing 31.6% of all students), whereas students taking exclusively distance education courses accounted for 3,003,080 people (14.9%) (Seaman et al., 2018). This shows that online education is no longer a trend; it is a reality. Institutions of higher education now consider online education a critical element of their long-term strategic planning; however, leadership still sees faculty acceptance showing only small signs of improvement.

Many instructors, older and with higher ranking, still tend to be reluctant to embrace online education. Some of the reasons for their resistance include the perception that online instruction gives few visual cues when interacting with learners, provides little interaction with and among learners, and is not as effective as in face-to-face classrooms when it comes to quality of content, among other reasons (Ubell, 2016). This lack of interaction and control over the teaching and learning experience fosters a feeling of impersonal instruction. Instructor resistance is mostly justified by unfamiliarity with online education, inexperience with online instruction, and lack of knowledge of online learning design (Conceição & Lehman, 2011).

In most online courses, instructors and learners are separated in time and space and depend on technology to facilitate interactions that often lack a strong personal dimension. As distance education programs continue to proliferate and mature, the emphasis on simply making content available to students online, emulating heavily text-based correspondence courses, is no longer acceptable. Yet, antiquated learning design practices persist in higher education and become amplified in online learning environments where technology-mediated communication combined with an emphasis on content delivery often ignores the personal dimension of learning. Creating online courses now requires a new way of thinking that incorporates new design ideas and approaches from a variety of fields; it also requires a new set of learning design skills for instructors and course designers.

The Focus of This Book

The focus of this book is on the learners and the design of their online learning experiences. We refer to learning design instead of instructional design—which focuses on instruction and places the instructor at the center stage of the process. Therefore, the focus is on approaching a learner's online course experience as a journey consisting of a combination of learning interactions with content, instructor, and other learners.

Who Can Benefit From This Book

This book provides instructors new to online course design with a holistic way of thinking about learners, learning, and online course design and distinctive strategies derived from an integrated framework for designing the online learning experience. This framework helps experienced instructors to intentionally use strategies for creating a holistic learning experience that is more personalized, engaging, and meaningful for online learners. These strategies are based on evidence-based learning design principles and strategies and allow readers of the book to adopt an empathic mindset focused on the experience of the learner.

For experienced online instructors and course designers, this book provides strategies for approaching the learning experience from an integrative perspective. The integrated framework for designing the online learning experience is not an instructional design model, nor is it intended to be a replacement for well-established learning design practices. Our approach to learning experience design attempts to supplement conventional learning design models and provides a set of principles and strategies intended to enhance and invigorate learning design practices for online courses. We encourage practitioners to continue using the learning design models they are most comfortable with that work in their context.

How the Book Is Organized

The book is organized into eight chapters. The opening chapter of the book, "Designing for the Learner Experience," addresses the changes in the dynamic learning ecosystem of higher education and the need for a unique mindset for designing learning for online environments. We explain why higher education is at a tipping point and the need to focus on learner-centered values and approaches in the online learning environment. We introduce concepts and research from a variety of fields, provide a definition of *learning experience design*, and offer core concepts that provide the basis for this book.

In chapter 2, "Integrated Framework for Designing the Online Learning Experience," we present several learner characteristics that can influence the design of online courses. Then we introduce the integrated framework for designing the online learning experience. The chapter concludes with a set of learning experience principles and strategies as a preparation for implementing the integrated framework in practice in subsequent chapters.

In chapter 3, "Designing the Course Structure and Learner Interface," we present common challenges and scenarios involved in designing a course structure and the impact of designing the learner interface on the learning experience. We conclude the chapter by presenting strategies for designing the online learning environment, applying design thinking and learner-centered design principles.

In chapter 4, "Facilitating Learning Through Instructional Content Design," we focus on the design of learner–content interactions and apply concepts and principles from the integrated framework for designing the online learning experience. The intent is to help instructors and course designers to adopt a learner-centered perspective for custom designing, curating external resources as well as repurposing and integrating content into the course structure and flow. We approach this design aspect by first defining what we mean by instructional content interactions and common starting points for designing online course content. We identify common challenges and design factors influencing instructional content design and present fundamental shifts in designing online content material. We conclude the chapter by offering practical strategies to enhance learner–content interactions and foster higher levels of engagement and deeper learning outcomes.

In chapter 5, "Creating Meaningful Learning Activities Through Learning Experience Design," we focus on the third design aspect. In this chapter, we describe key attributes and types of online learning activities. The emphasis throughout this chapter is on applying design thinking as a foundational strategy for creating innovative learning solutions. We provide an example scenario for creating online learning activities using the design thinking process. We conclude the chapter with strategies for designing online learning activities.

In chapter 6, "Enhancing Motivation, Engagement, and Learning Through Social Interactions," we build on learner–content interactions and focus on the fourth design aspect: social interactions that derive from technology-mediated interpersonal communication between learner and instructor and learners with other learners. In this chapter, we explain why social interactions matter, highlight types of social interactions, identify five factors influencing the design of social interactions, provide a process for designing social interactions, and suggest strategies for integrating social interactions into learning experience design.

In chapter 7, "Incorporating Assessments and Feedback Throughout the Learning Experience," we focus on the last design aspect: assessments and feedback. In this chapter, we differentiate between assessments and feedback, provide ways for rethinking assessments and feedback as learning experiences, and provide strategies for incorporating assessments and feedback into learning experience design. We highlight the importance of incorporating assessments and feedback into the learning experience to sustain learners' attention and motivation.

Chapters 3 through 7 begin with guiding design questions. These questions are answered in the chapters by providing strategies as design solutions. These chapters focus on enhancing online learning experiences for each of the major aspects of an online course, providing evidence-based principles and strategies to promote learner engagement and deep learning.

In chapter 8, "Putting It Together," we provide an example illustrating a real-world application of the principles and strategies covered in the book using design thinking to create learning experiences. We also provide a summary of the guiding design questions and design strategies for each design aspect in the integrated framework for designing the online learning experience. We conclude with approaches for moving forward for designing the online learning experience.

Our Design Thinking Process for Writing This Book

With similar experiences but different backgrounds in learning design, we brought diverse perspectives into the writing of this book. Conceição is a scholar-practitioner whereas Howles is a practitioner-scholar. Writing this book involved an iterative process. We did not use a linear approach for writing one chapter after the other; instead, we brainstormed ideas, sketched concepts, developed outlines, created graphics, and then put those ideas into a written format. We used design thinking and a free-flow style that required an open mind for accepting new ideas and perspectives. Often we needed to process these ideas on our own or through ongoing exploration of the literature for a couple of days before settling in with a concept to build a chapter.

The first chapter begins with examining concepts and research from a variety of fields—user experience design, human factors design, human-centered design, and design thinking. These concepts served as the foundation for the entire book. Our intention was to bring together concepts to create innovative ideas to solve design challenges. Other design concepts emerged as we moved forward with the subsequent chapters; however, we often returned to the first two chapters to add or remove concepts as our thinking became more refined upon sharing our sketches with stakeholders (learners, instructors, and course designers) and discussing between ourselves. The iterative process was essential for our writing.

The integrated framework for designing the online learning experience emerged and evolved through the iterative process and design thinking. Once we established the framework in chapter 2, chapters 3 to 7, on the design aspects of the framework, were created by building on each other's concepts, principles, and strategies, always focusing on the learner experience in an online course. These five chapters could not have been created as stand-alone sections since the online learning experience is holistic and requires flow.

One important element of our writing process was to apply our new design ideas in practice. The integrated framework for designing the online learning experience was employed in a course taught by Conceição in spring 2019. This allowed for rapid prototyping of our new ideas, receiving feedback on areas that were unclear, and reality checking. Rapid prototyping of our work proved to be valuable for putting it together. The final chapter shows how the ideas in this book can be brought together using the concepts, principles, and strategies provided in this book.

For us, empathic design, always keeping the learner perspective in mind when designing aspects of an online course, is paramount. The learner perspective is in the forefront of making design decisions. Using design thinking and an iterative process was like putting into practice what we are advocating in this book. We hope this book inspires instructors and course designers to reinvigorate their current practices and ways of thinking about online learning design in their own contexts and build on the ideas from this book.

Simone C.O. Conceição, PhD
Milwaukee, Wisconsin

Les L. Howles, MS
Waunakee, Wisconsin

I

DESIGNING FOR THE LEARNER EXPERIENCE

Higher education has gone through major shifts in the last few decades. These shifts are the result of enrollment decline, changes in learner demographics, and skills expectations of employers. These changes have driven innovation and the need for a shift from emphasizing instruction and content to designing impactful learning experiences for a more diverse, mobile, and tech-savvy student population. With a learner population that is more diverse, mobile, and technologically savvy, the design of these experiences requires a different mindset that places greater attention on the overall experience of learners. This chapter explains why higher education is at a tipping point and the need to focus on learner-centered values and approaches, particularly in the online learning environment. We introduce concepts and research from a variety of fields, provide a definition of *learning experience design*, and offer core concepts that provide the basis for this book.

Tipping Point in Higher Education

The context of higher education in the United States is at a tipping point due to enrollment changes, shifts in student demographics, the continued rise in college tuition, the need to prepare a workforce with new skills, and the struggle to deal with innovation. These changes have led to the rise of online education and the need to focus on how learning is designed and delivered in a time in which the value of education is at stake.

Overall U.S. higher education enrollments in brick-and-mortar institutions continue to decline, whereas online education enrollments continue to grow (Seaman et al., 2018). This trend has made online educational offerings part of the norm for many higher education institutions. The shift in student demographics shows that nontraditional students are the new majority of postsecondary enrollment. The profile of these students is 25 years old or older, with full-time jobs and family obligations, likely attending school on a part-time basis (Dabbagh, 2007) and choosing online education as their primary mode of learning.

At the time of the publication of this book, many of these nontraditional students were millennials, those aged 26 to 35 years in 2016 (Fry, 2016), accustomed to highly personalized phones and computers (Twenge, 2014). Millennial learners have encountered the most rapid changes in terms of technology, have spent their entire lives surrounded by and using technologies (Rosen, 2011), and have different educational expectations involving technology. Their learning readiness and preparedness for the use of technology place new demands on higher education to innovate.

With high expectations from millennials for an immediate return on investment (ROI) after graduation and the continued rise in college tuition with no guarantee that a diploma will lead to a job, the value of higher education is being questioned. With a particular set of priorities, students are now doing their own search for courses and programs that provide value for their education (Weise & Christensen, 2014). Value means a learning experience that is flexible, convenient, relevant, and affordable and that provides the skills needed to be a highly functional member of the workforce.

Employers also have higher expectations for developing a more skilled workforce. They are demanding graduates with academic credentials that reflect specific proficiencies and skills related to industry needs. However, increasingly higher education is perceived as not preparing students to meet these needs and students want their education to more directly connect with employer needs, such that learning and work become inseparable twins (Weise & Christensen, 2014).

All these changes drive higher education institutions to innovate and act in new ways. Institutions that fail to innovate will be left behind. Institutions that are dealing with these changes are going through mergers within a university system (Savidge, 2017), adopting blended and online delivery approaches (Bowen, 2012), using mastery and modularization of learning to meet learner demands (Weise & Christensen, 2014), and moving to competency-based education and online learning (University of Wisconsin System, 2018). This, however, is not enough. Instructors and course designers, who have the greatest impact on the learner experience, must also embrace these changes. These changes require not only an awareness of the present context of higher education but also a recognition of the current dynamic learning ecosystem and a unique mindset for designing learning.

Dynamic Learning Ecosystem

Emerging technologies have influenced how a person thinks, feels, and behaves in a learning environment. Learning has become part of a much bigger, more dynamic digital ecosystem; it is now taking place everywhere—in libraries, on the internet, in books, and on digital devices—and no longer occurs in the vacuum of a traditional classroom setting. New digital learning environments integrate content, technology, and people within an institutional culture (Rosenberg & Foreman, 2014). Content is administrated and managed centrally through an institution and can also be social, collaboratively administered, and expert-generated. This ecosystem is mediated by technology, which extends the processes and functions of learning, yet all of this does not guarantee learning success. The culture involves the university, business, and communities of practice.

In this dynamic learning ecosystem, learners have access to experts such as instructors who facilitate their learning and encourage them to take responsibility for their own learning. In technology-enabled online and blended courses, learning can be designed as an experience, part of a dynamic process, rather than a series of required tasks and assignments. Social networking and collaboration are integral components of this learning process (Rosenberg & Foreman, 2014).

In this learning ecosystem, instructors take on multiple roles—learning designer, evaluator, observer, supporter, facilitator, and mentor (Lehman & Conceição, 2010). Though studies have shown that some instructors in traditional higher education environments tend to focus mainly on teaching and content (Bennett et al., 2017; Postareff & Lindblom-Ylänne, 2008), in a dynamic learning ecosystem, this mindset is counterproductive. The practice of making content available online to learners, replicating heavily content-based instruction, is not congruent with a dynamic learning environment and the learner characteristics of today. This shift in perspective requires a whole new way of thinking about course design.

Mindset Shift for Designing Learning

As instructors and course designers embark on learning design for the online environment, there are new ways of thinking about the learner, the environment, and learning interactions. Designing online learning in this digital age requires a mindset that places a greater emphasis on how learners respond cognitively, emotionally, behaviorally, and socially in a dynamic learning ecosystem. Creating new types of learning experiences requires an open mind and an exploratory attitude toward using innovative technologies. Learning design is no longer a solitary task performed by a subject matter expert; it involves continuous and in-depth feedback from a variety of stakeholders throughout the online course design process. Most of all, it requires a shift from a content-focused delivery mindset to a learner-centered approach focused on the learning experience in a holistic way.

The Learner-Centered Approach in Higher Education

The concept of a learner-centered approach has been a major theme in educational psychology research since the 1990s. Several learner-centered principles have been developed that focus the design of learning from the perspective of the learner. These principles view the learner and the learning process holistically, recognizing that learning environments interact with various internal factors of learners. These internal psychological factors center on cognitive, affective, developmental, social, and other individual differences that address the learner and the learning process in the context of real-world learning situations (Learner-Centered Principles Workgroup, 1997).

When initially developed, these principles served as a framework for learner-centered educational practices, with the purpose of positively impacting student learning outcomes and satisfaction (Learner-Centered Principles Workgroup, 1997). Using these principles ensures greater connection and empathy with learners at multiple levels—intellectual, emotional, social, and behavioral.

Learner-centered design principles have been applied to online learning contexts for a few reasons. Technology-mediated environments have been viewed as less personal, and so there is a need for greater learner engagement. Learners are not in close proximity to instructors and often feel a sense of disconnectedness. Because the online learning context presents constraints in how students interact with content, instructors, and other learners, it becomes important to consider these challenges and potential solutions when designing online courses.

Design of Online Learning Environments

New technologies and media have given rise to next-generation digital learning environments and learning ecosystems to support both blended and online learning (Brown et al., 2015). Accompanying the development of new technology-enabled learning spaces is an emerging concern about becoming overly technology-focused. Some learning ecosystem models in higher education focus heavily on technical infrastructure, increased functionality, interoperability, and integration of tools and software using a learning management system (LMS) to support both on-campus and online instruction (Kellen, 2017). However, these systems often impose limitations for the design of learning. Rosenberg and Foreman (2014) criticized many digital learning environments as being overly technology-centric. Technology-centric approaches begin by focusing on the features and functional capabilities of new tools and then look toward finding ways they can be used to transmit subject matter, often with limited input from instructors and learners.

Nielsen (2017) has noted that all too often the adoption of new technologies typically moves us one step forward in terms of new capabilities but often takes us back two steps in terms of usability and human factors. In this book, we advocate and envision new designs for learning environments that are learner-centered from the ground up. It is helpful to look to other disciplines for inspiration, new approaches, and ideas for designing more learner-centered approaches to technology-enhanced learning.

Inspiration From Other Disciplines

One field to note is human factors research and design, which specializes in designing technology for human use (Huchingson, 1981). This field emerged from the recognition that instead of adapting technology to the needs of humans, humans were often forced to adapt to the design features of technology-based systems and tools. The goal of human factors research was to study and improve human interaction with technology-enabled systems, particularly with computers. Initially, considerable attention was placed on the design of user/computer interfaces and how users interacted with them to perform tasks. Over time, the term *human-centered design* became one of the mantras for the human factors design community (Norman, 2005).

In the 1990s, Don Norman took the human-centered design concept one step further and coined the term *user experience design* (UXD). UXD goes beyond a focus on functionality, usefulness, efficiency, and what people see and do on computer screens (Nielsen, 2017). In the broadest sense, the scope of UXD encompasses any interaction with any product, artifact, or system focusing on people's needs, reactions, and behaviors. Garrett (2011) highlighted the user-centered aspect of UXD as taking "the user into account every step of the way" (p. 17) while developing a product.

As a process, UXD incorporates all activities from inception to implementation of a product or service. It is a holistic design approach encompassing the sum total of what's happening to the user of a product or service. It includes affective elements such as user engagement, enjoyment, and satisfaction. It balances user needs with the needs and goals of the organization (Garrett, 2011). In education, particularly in the area of designing technology-based learning environments, we are approaching a similar situation. There are many similarities between learner-centered design and user-centered design in terms of values, processes, and outcomes.

Learner Experience Design

The design of online education has much in common and much to learn from UXD. In the field of UXD, the term *experience* is a key transformational concept (Garrett, 2011). The emphasis goes beyond creating a functional, efficient, and usable product or service, but instead an overall positive and memorable user experience.

Learning experiences are highly subjective psychodynamic states resulting from a person's combined interactions with course content, instructors, fellow learners, and various media and technologies involved in the learning process. To have a "learning experience," learners are deeply invested at the cognitive, emotional, social, and behavioral levels. According to Kolb and Kolb (2009), "Learning is a holistic process of adaptation. It is not just the result of cognition but involves the integrated functioning of the total person—thinking, feeling, perceiving, and behaving" (p. 43).

Experience design coupled with learner-centered design aims to engage learners at deeper and more personal levels as participants in the learning process, creating experiences that span course, unit, and lesson levels. Whether intentional or not, every online course, lesson, learning activity, or content resource reflects design decisions that impact the learner's experience in some way.

The design of a well-crafted and impactful learning experience is an appealing goal for instructors and course designers but in practice is seldom well thought out and fully acted upon. Common design strategies for online courses rely heavily on LMSs. They enable rapid course development through the use of templates, list-based content menus, links to discussion forums, and student tracking. These environments are not learner-centered by design, but instead focus on institutional and instructor course management needs. Many LMSs inadvertently encourage content-centric design, a one-size-fits-all course structure, and a passive learning design mindset.

Learner experience design emphasizes learner-centered values and principles in all aspects of online course design, including user interfaces, content presentations, learning activities, social interactions, and assessments and feedback in the design of learning at the course, lesson, and learning activity levels.

Learner experience design is becoming more relevant as new digital pedagogies and technologies become incorporated into online courses. These technologies include open educational resources (OERs), personalized learning, adaptive learning, games and simulations, and immersive technologies such as augmented and virtual reality. Learner experience design ensures that next-generation digital learning environments and ecosystems put the learner at the center and technology in the background, to better serve the needs and goals of learners and instructors.

Our Definition of Learning Experience Design

Learning experience design focuses on the structure and psychodynamics of individual and group experiences that take place in the context of a particular learning environment. In this book, we approach learning experience design as a process and set of principles that involve creating technology-mediated interactions applied at the course, lesson, and activity levels in the online environment. Experience design is holistic in that it integrates the cognitive, emotional, behavioral, and social dimensions of learning. Figure 1.1 depicts the four dimensions of learning and how they serve as a foundation for the learning experience.

The *cognitive dimension* is the realm of mental activities and processes that includes perception, memory, classification, reasoning, critical thinking, and problem-solving. Within the cognitive dimension, learning is often viewed in terms of content acquisition, knowledge construction, and building intellectual skills (Anderson & Krathwohl, 2001).

Figure 1.1. Dimensions of learning.

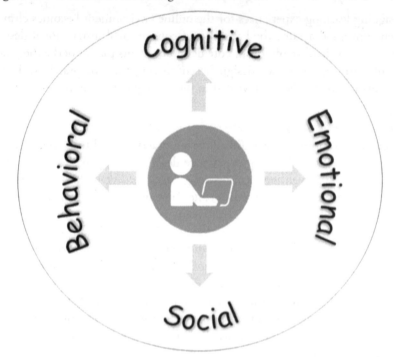

The *emotional dimension* is closely associated with learner motivation and encompasses both positive and negative emotions. Although learners may desire their learning experiences to be enjoyable and engaging, most meaningful and deep learning experiences often involve episodes of confusion, frustration, and struggle before positive feelings of accomplishment emerge (D'Mello et al., 2014; Graesser & D'Mello, 2011).

The *social dimension* focuses on the relationship and discourse between individuals in a learning environment. Unlike the other three dimensions, which are essential for almost all types of learning, meaningful and deep learning through social interaction needs to be approached more judiciously, and sometimes it may not need to be a core component in the design of every learning experience.

The *behavioral dimension* is an extension and externalization of the other three dimensions. It bridges the knowing–doing gap by connecting knowledge construction with application. Behavior is shaped and supported through thinking, feeling, and social interactions. In addition, how learners self-regulate their own learning process through decisions and choices manifests in their behaviors throughout a course experience (Cazan, 2013).

Core Concepts for Learning Experience Design

Designing learning experiences for the online environment becomes clearer when contrasted against the backdrop of conventional instructional design practices. For that, we offer four core design concepts that underlie the practice of learning experience design by comparing the two practices. These concepts will be frequently revisited in the subsequent chapters.

Learner-Centered Design

Whereas conventional instructional design practices tend to be instruction- and content-centric, learning experience design focuses on the learner and learning tasks. Conventional course design decisions focus almost exclusively on the learner's cognitive dimension and these decisions are usually made by the instructor without feedback from learners.

Learner experience design puts a greater effort toward viewing each aspect of the online course environment from the perspective of a learner and does this by applying the four dimensions of learning as a lens for envisioning the learning experience. Using this approach, instructors and course designers can avoid the tendency of using their own personal perspectives and assumptions about learners when making design decisions. By communicating and listening to learners before, during, and after the course regarding how they are thinking, feeling, and responding to the course, instructors and course designers can gain a better sense of the experience from the learner's point of view. Learning objectives and course content can remain the same, but instructors gain insights to reshape elements of the course design based on the expressed mental, emotional, behavioral, and social needs of learners. This approach requires a type of openness and empathy (caring and curiosity) to understand the spoken and unspoken needs of learners and how they react to different aspects of the online course experience.

Emotional Design

Most conventional instructional design practices tend to overlook the emotional dimension of learning in the online environment. In contrast, online learning experience design focuses on the tight integration of cognition and emotions in learning. There are deep connections between cognition, affect, motivation, and social interactions. The design of learning experiences takes these connections into consideration in a holistic way. The emotional dimension of learning is of greater importance when learning goals involve complex content and deep learning (Graesser & D'Mello, 2011). Emotional design for learning may deliberately evoke both positive and negative emotions that, if managed, can result in more impactful learning experiences. These include a range of emotions. When deep learning of complex material is a goal, periods of confusion, frustration, and anxiety can serve as antecedents in producing positive states such as delight, challenge, flow, and surprise.

Participatory Design

The conventional course development process is heavily reliant on a single subject matter expert's decision regarding how a learning experience will be designed and their assumptions about how learners will respond. Collaboration and participation of others in the design process is often seen as unnecessary and time-consuming. Although the instructional design process for online courses has become less insular by involving technical and instructional design support, it still leaves out many stakeholders in making design decisions, particularly those who are destined to take the course.

The field of participatory design for human–computer systems is based on a central principle that users of any system should have input into its design (DiSalvo et al., 2017; Schuler & Namioka, 1993). Participatory design involves input and feedback from multiple stakeholders throughout the design process. The goal is that the design of online learning experiences will benefit from a greater number and type of inputs compared to conventional courses (Welsh & Dehler, 2012). Learning experience design involves collaboration among learners, instructors, and course designers in the online course design process to ensure the needs of learners are addressed. In this case, the traditional role of the instructor at the center of the course design process shifts and expands to include the role of managing the collaborative design process. Input from learners is solicited during various phases of the course design process (Könings et al., 2014). The goal is to reinstate the learner as a central figure in the learning design process. To do this effectively requires a special type of mindset, often referred to as *design thinking*.

Design Thinking
The concept of design thinking, although now widely applied in multiple disciplines, has no single agreed-upon definition; it is typically used as a problem-solving approach for understanding and generating innovative solutions for complex problems. Design thinking has been presented as a mindset, a problem-solving process, a set of principles, and a toolkit for developing innovative products and services (Brenner et al., 2016). Over the last few years, there has been a growing awareness that the methods and thinking used behind great designs in engineering, architecture, health care, industrial design, and other professions can be applied in education, particularly for designing learning experiences (Koh et al., 2015).

Design thinking is a term we use to denote the ability to adapt and incorporate design thinking processes, principles, and practices into designing aspects of online courses. Design thinking can be not only applied to the creation of an entire online course environment but also used in a granular way in designing smaller scale but critical learning experiences, including content interactions, instructor communication, social interactions, and learning activities. It becomes particularly useful in situations where an instructor is interested in developing innovative technology-based learning solutions.

Design thinking reinvigorates conventional instructional design practices and is well suited for working with new technologies and learning ecosystems. Instructors and course designers can better utilize affordances of new learning technologies to craft more learner-centered, engaging, and meaningful online course experiences. Design thinking embodies concepts such as empathy, collaboration, ideation, prototyping, and user testing and incorporates these as practices in the learning design process. Our emphasis throughout this book is to approach design thinking more as a mindset and toolkit that instructors and course designers can adapt to their situational needs rather than as a procedure or recipe to follow.

Integrating Design Thinking Into Learning Experience Design

A key feature of design thinking is its human-centered and experience-focused orientation (Brown, 2009), which aligns with a learner-centered approach to the design of online courses and learning experiences. A learning experience begins the moment learners enter an online course environment and continues as they interact with content, people, and technology in the learning space. Instructors and course designers of online learning environments shape the quality of the learner experience; however, they are not always able to see, hear, and experience the course from the perspective of a learner. Too often instructors and course designers envision an online course from the inside out, focusing on the content that goes inside the learning environment. An outside-in approach focuses on the learners' perspective as they engage and interact with content and every other aspect of the learning environment. The ability to let go of one's own preconceptions and personal preferences and look at an online course's content and structure from a learner perspective is not easy. Doing this involves a core design thinking skill, which we refer to as *empathic design*.

Design thinking incorporates and puts into practice participatory design. Coming to closure too rapidly on important course design decisions is discouraged, along with insular decision-making by one individual. Instead, design thinking encourages continuous collaboration and feedback from peer instructors, former and prospective learners, and other colleagues involved in course design and delivery.

Good designers are continuously running their ideas by others, getting feedforward before investing in building anything substantial, rapidly iterating and vetting their ideas. Designing learning experiences is a process of successive approximation which the skilled course designer moves through rapidly. It is about letting go of "functional fixedness"—a type of cognitive bias that drives people to use both existing and new tools in standard ways (Harley, 2017).

Whereas conventional design decision-making for classroom-based courses tends to adopt the first idea generated by the instructor or course designer, learning experience design looks for new and better ways of designing learning experiences in all aspects of a course. The first idea is seldom the last idea that gets implemented. It involves an experimentation mindset using rapid prototyping to test out new ideas. It explores new approaches and reality tests them quickly, involving both feedforward and feedback.

Design thinking as a process involves several key practices that we refer to throughout this book:

1. *Empathize with learners* by constantly keeping the learner perspective in mind and even seeking their ideas and feedback when making important design decisions. Remember the four Cs when practicing empathic design:

    a. Caring about the learner's experience

    b. Curiosity about how learners are thinking, feeling, behaving, and talking about their learning experiences

    c. Conversations with learners to better understand their course experiences

    d. Changing or correcting deficiencies in the course design based on learner needs, suggestions, and feedback

2. *Define design challenge(s)* by conducting research, observing activities, and collecting input from stakeholders (learners). This requires deferring coming up with solutions, instead asking lots of questions to fully understand design issues from multiple perspectives. This also requires curiosity by asking why, how, what, who, and when questions.

3. *Ideate and brainstorm a variety of potential solutions* on how to address the learning design challenge for innovative solutions. This involves collaborating with others to envision and generate a variety of "what-if" ideas while keeping focused on the design challenge and the learner perspective. This usually involves sketches that bring cloudy ideas into a more tangible form.

4. *Prototype ideas* by making one or two of the best potential solutions more tangible through rough mockups, visual narratives, or storyboards showing how learners might interact with the solution. These prototypes require minimal investment and can be quickly refined through successive iteration based on stakeholder feedback.

5. *Test design solutions* by refining prototype designs and returning to learners and other stakeholders for validation of a final design. This may also involve pilot testing a design solution in the context of a real course and obtaining feedback.

6. *Implement the final design*, ensuring that people, technologies, and processes are fully in place and the newly designed solution is achieving its intended goals. Because our focus is on the design, this phase will not be further addressed.

We view design thinking as an integral part of learning experience design. Our aim is to enable effective practice of design thinking within a narrower and somewhat unique context. We apply design thinking in an adaptive and flexible method in the context of online learning.

What Is Next for Instructors and Course Designers

As the learning ecosystem in higher education evolves, so do the practices of instructors and course designers who genuinely care about the learner experience in an online environment. Learning experience design is a learner-centered approach requiring a different mindset, process, and toolkit for instructors and course designers. Chapter 2 introduces the integrated framework for designing the online learning experience, which supplements the core concepts introduced in this chapter.

2

INTEGRATED FRAMEWORK
FOR DESIGNING THE
ONLINE LEARNING
EXPERIENCE

The notion that individuals have "learning experiences" is not new. What is new, however, is a growing interest in "designing" learning experiences. Compared to conventional instructional design, crafting quality online learning involves a shift in the way we think about and develop courses. This shift entails a more holistic and learner-centered way of designing learning for a digital age. We refer to this new mindset and approach as *learning experience design*.

In this chapter, we introduce the integrated framework for designing the online learning experience. Practicing learning experience design requires empathic design and a deeper understanding of the learner perspective. We begin this chapter by looking at several learner characteristics that can influence the design of learning experiences. This chapter includes a set of design principles and strategies as preparation for implementing the integrated framework in practice in subsequent chapters.

Learner Characteristics

Learning experiences within individual learners are highly subjective. What each person brings to a learning situation influences the quality of the experience. Therefore, designing online learning experiences requires a more in-depth understanding of learner traits compared to a conventional instructional design target audience analysis. Learner characteristics represent individual differences that impact internal conditions of learning (Gagne &

Figure 2.1. Learner characteristics that influence learning design.

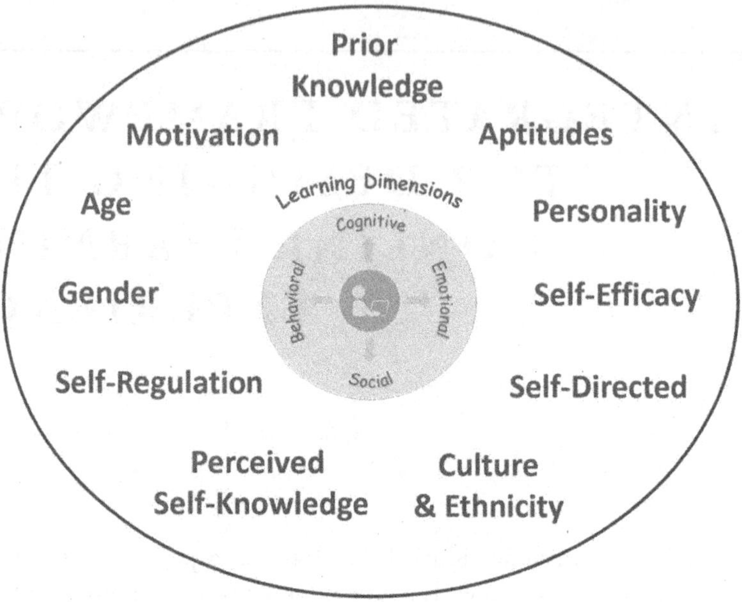

Briggs, 1979). Experience design involves recognizing how these individual differences interact with various aspects of the online course environment. Figure 2.1 shows 11 evidence-based learner characteristics that impact how learners engage cognitively, emotionally, behaviorally, and socially in an online environment.

Prior Knowledge

Prior knowledge is associated with the cognitive dimension of learning. It is an individual's stored knowledge from previous learning experiences. This knowledge is represented in the brain in the form of neural networks (Zull, 2002) or cognitive structures called *schemas* (Sweller, 1994). Individuals have schemas for objects, events, and ideas. Schemas help individuals recognize and describe things. Existing schemas provide a structure for organizing new information (Jonassen et al., 1993) and also serve as catalysts for making thinking and learning more efficient. Learning and meaning-making involve building new schemas and expanding existing ones. Prior knowledge in the form of schemas is one of the greatest factors in predicting a learner's initial success in a learning situation.

Learner-centered design involves recognizing that individual learners differ in terms of their prior knowledge and schemas. Instructional methods need to adapt to learner differences in prior knowledge (Clark et al., 2006). Course content that may seem simple and straightforward to learners with prior knowledge may be confusing to others whose schemas related to that content are not well formed. Low prior knowledge learners require more redundancy, structure, explicitness, and external support when first exposed to new and complex content. As learners acquire greater expertise, the amount of structure, explicitness, and support decreases.

Motivation

Motivation is closely associated with the emotional dimension of learning but is also intertwined with a person's thinking and behavior. Motivation acts as an internal force that activates, directs, and sustains an individual's attention and behaviors toward achieving certain goals. It influences choices, effort, and persistence. It also underlies a person's level of engagement in performing learning tasks and sets the stage for deep learning to occur. The amount of mental effort invested in a learning task is a reliable estimate of the learner's motivation or involvement in the task (Paas et al., 2005).

Because of the complexities of different learning situations, there is no single formula for motivating all learners. An individual's motivation to learn is influenced by both internal (intrinsic) and external (extrinsic) factors. Intrinsic motivation involves a personal interest and desire to engage in a task, whereas extrinsic motivation involves an outside demand that may include reinforcements, rewards, punishments, or other consequences. Although activating a learner's intrinsic motivation is an ideal goal, a mix of intrinsic and extrinsic motivation should be incorporated in an online course design. Online content and learning activity design need to build in elements of learner interest, relevance, practical application, and challenge.

Self-Regulation

Self-regulation is a set of metacognitive strategies associated with the behavioral, cognitive, and emotional dimensions of learning. It is the degree to which students are "metacognitively, motivationally, and behaviorally active participants in their own learning process" (Zimmerman & Martinez-Pons, 1988, p. 284). Metacognitive strategies are adopted by learners to monitor, plan, and regulate their learning. Motivation is a sustainer of self-regulation. Self-regulated learners in the online environment tend to be more confident and more engaged in the learning process, with better performance on tests (Puzziferro, 2008). Learning online requires more self-regulation due to the independent nature of the work. Broadbent and Poon (2015) stated,

Students who make good use of their time, are conscious of their learning behavior, are critical in their examination of content and persevere in understanding the learning material despite challenges faced are more likely to achieve higher academic grades in online settings. (p. 11)

Self-Directed

Self-directedness is the learner's ability to guide and direct their own learning with moral, emotional, and intellectual autonomy (Song & Hill, 2007). This learner characteristic is closely associated with the emotional, cognitive, behavioral, and social dimensions of learning. As a personal attribute, self-directedness has been presented from different perspectives. Candy's (1991) perspective encompasses personal autonomy, self-management, and learner control. Brockett and Hiemstra (1991) viewed self-directed as a personal responsibility orientation (goal and process), in which goal orientation centers on "a learner's desire or preference for assuming responsibility for learning" (p. 24). Garrison's (1997) personal attribute involves three dimensions interacting with each other: learners' control of learning context to reach learning objectives (self-management), use of learning resources within the learning context (self-monitoring), and motivation to learn.

The demands of many online courses require learners to be self-determined and self-directed in how they interact with peers and the instructor, communicate with others in a timely manner following established guidelines, and become motivated to participate in meaningful interactions providing thoughtful in-depth contributions. In order to be successful in the online learning environment, learners need to take control over their own learning, be self-motivated, and manage deadlines (Song & Hill, 2007), all of which constitute self-directed learning readiness (Boyer et al., 2006; Kreber, 2004).

Self-Efficacy

Self-efficacy is the personal belief held by learners regarding how well they can perform a task (Bandura, 1997; Huffman et al., 2013). This learner characteristic is linked to the emotional, cognitive, and behavioral dimensions of learning. Learners' self-efficacy shapes their motivation and the particular learning strategies they employ in relation to a specific learning context or activity. When learners feel reasonably confident about reaching a particular goal or accomplishing a particular task, they generally put forth their best effort. Students' effort and motivation often decline in learning situations where they feel incapable.

Low self-efficacy fosters a tendency toward procrastination, which is amplified in an online learning environment. Self-efficacy is difficult to discern in online environments, but lack of self-efficacy is evident when students procrastinate. Procrastinators have difficulty with tactics such as organizing resources and managing tasks for short-term goals. They devote too much time to the wrong tasks and tend to delay the start of long-term tasks (Klassen et al., 2008).

Perceived Self-Knowledge

One characteristic closely associated with the cognitive dimension is an individual's ability to accurately self-judge their knowledge of a specific topic and self-assess their own learning (calibration). It is a metacognitive ability that can be measured in specific learning situations. Accurate self-assessments of one's learning plays a key role in the learning process. If students have inaccurate self-judgments regarding what they have learned and where they need to improve, they will be less capable of effectively guiding and self-regulating their own learning (Dunlosky et al., 2005).

There is a type of inflated overconfidence related to a person's judgment accuracy of what they have learned following a learning event (Dunlosky & Rawson, 2012). Older individuals show a tendency toward greater overconfidence compared to younger individuals (Crawford & Stankov, 1996). Overall, learners tend to hold overly optimistic and miscalibrated views about their acquired learning, which become even more miscalibrated and overconfident when people face difficult tasks—ones for which they fail to possess prerequisite knowledge—than ones for which they do possess that knowledge. Online learners also express preferences for learning methods based on their enjoyment of the learning experience; these often may not be the optimal methods for achieving learning outcomes (Graesser & D'Mello, 2011).

Personality

Personality indicates individual differences in long-standing patterns in the way a person thinks, feels, and behaves. Personality traits have been found to influence individual behaviors in a variety of academic contexts including online courses. The big five personality model has classified five traits to identify the underlying personality structure of individuals: extraversion, emotional stability, conscientiousness, agreeableness, and openness to experience (Costa & McCrae, 1992). Every individual has all five traits in various levels or tendencies.

Cohen and Baruth (2017) looked at personality traits driving learner satisfaction in an online environment and found conscientiousness and openness to experience to be the most dominant. Conscientious students are likely to meet deadlines for assignments, finish tasks rather than leave them incomplete, put a considerable amount of effort into a task, and apply themselves without continuous supervision (Crozier, 1997). Students exhibiting an openness to experience tend to be intellectually curious, interested in course material, and insightful, all of which contribute to better course performance (Hazrati-Viari et al., 2012). Learners who are more conscientious and open to experience may require less instructional support and external regulation, less human or computerized feedback, and less coaching. It is just the opposite for learners with a less conscientious personality type.

Age

The online learner population is becoming more heterogenous and intergenerational. A typical course might include part-time working adults who are goal-oriented and young full-time students who are self-directed. Instructors and course designers need to create online learning experiences that accommodate a wide range of age differences. A popular trend is the use of generational classification terms such as *digital natives, digital immigrants, millennials,* or *gen Xers.* However, researchers studying age differences and learning advise against this type of categorization and instead focus on identifying specific generational learner characteristics. Though significant generational distinctions or categories that clearly set apart learners based on digital competencies have not yet been identified (Gallardo-Echenique et al., 2015), there is solid evidence of pronounced psychological differences in learner traits between younger and older learners.

There are two streams of research focusing on age differences and academic performance, with implications for the behavioral, emotional, and cognitive dimensions of learning in the online environment: technology utilization and learning capabilities and performance. Age-related technology utilization research shows that there are significant and practical differences in technology use between individuals based on age and time period in which they were born (Gallardo-Echenique et al., 2015; Lai & Hong, 2015). Contrary to popular belief, younger students tend not to use digital technologies more extensively than older students for learning purposes (Bullen et al., 2011; Jelfs & Richardson, 2013). However, learning capabilities and performance differences between older and younger learners are attributable to age-related changes, such as decline in certain mental faculties as people age and manifest differences in technology-related learning tasks.

As individuals age, there are gradual cognitive, emotional, and motivational changes that can vary widely from person to person. Older learners require more time to perform tasks (Wolfson et al., 2014). Starting in the early 30s, there is a gradual reduction in cognitive processing speed, often related to a steady reduction of working memory capacity.

As individuals begin approaching middle age, they gradually become more negatively impacted by information overload. In addition, older adults experience greater difficulty learning novel material for which they have no existing prior knowledge or schemas. The greater the task complexity, the greater the performance gap between younger and older adults (Oberauer & Kliegl, 2001; Salthouse, 1992). In addition, there are declines with age in executive functioning controlling attention, as well as the processing and integration of new information. Younger learners' executive functions are still in development whereas older adult learners' spatial abilities have begun to decline, particularly those related to large-scale spatial tasks and navigation (Schoenfeld et al., 2010). This has implications for navigating complex virtual spaces.

Culture and Ethnicity

Cultural dispositions and norms associated with learner ethnicity groups constitute an influence mediated by individual difference that can shape a learner's overall experience in online contexts. According to the National Center for Education Statistics, the growing diversity of American college students has shifted, with the proportion of White students decreasing and the number of students belonging to other racial/ethnic groups rising (Snyder & Dillow, 2011). Studies comparing perceptions of students across different ethnic and cultural groups reveal differences in students' perceptions and experiences of online learning.

Cultural differences have been found to impact individual preferences and satisfaction with online learning (Ke, 2010). Many ethnic minority students report fewer positive perceptions and satisfaction with online courses compared to White students (Ke & Kwak, 2013; Xu & Jaggars, 2013). Ethnic groups coming from high-context or collectivist cultural orientations have been found to differ from groups with an individualistic cultural norm. High-context groups include Native Americans, Hispanics, East Asians, and African Americans.

Aptitudes

An aptitude is a natural inborn talent or ability enabling an individual to perform certain types of work or tasks easily and quickly. It is one of the strongest individual characteristics influencing a learner's competency in performing certain types of instructional tasks. Examples of aptitudes that can be measured include numerical, visual/spatial, verbal/linguistic, kinesthetic, and artistic/musical. Students with high aptitudes in certain areas often show a quicker initial understanding of certain content and tasks. Aptitude has little association with prior knowledge, cultural background, education, or motivation.

Aptitude has implications for the design of online courses and is associated with all four dimensions of learning. For example, learners with higher visual-spatial abilities tend to outperform those with lower visual-spatial abilities while learning with complex visual representations. High spatial ability students benefit more from certain types of visual displays that combine words and pictorial information (Brucker et al., 2014; Mayer & Sims, 1994). There is a need to be sensitive that students in online courses are likely to possess a range of aptitudes related to learning certain types of content and skills. Struggling motivated students can achieve these competencies but may require additional support, encouragement, and scaffolding.

Gender

Research on gender differences related to learning are mixed and are often hotly debated as to whether differences can be attributed to cultural or inborn factors. There is no evidence that there is a distinct male and female brain. There appear to be a few gender differences that can impact online learning, but it is important to keep in mind that there are wide variances between individuals within a gender under the influence of cultural norms and tendencies. It is best to view any apparent gender characteristics as a mosaic of attributes that are shared by both males and females in diverse proportions, with unlimited variation at the individual level.

Studies comparing learning outcomes, performance, and satisfaction between male and female students in the online environment are mixed. Studies have shown that females, compared to males, participate more in online discussions and engage more actively in online learning tasks than male counterparts (Chang et al., 2014). Xu and Jaggars (2013), in examining over 12,000 community college students, found that men had more difficulty adapting to online learning than did women, and although females outperformed their male counterparts on average across all courses, the gender performance gap was stronger in the online context than in the face-to-face context.

Compared to females, males tend to have higher levels of confidence and self-efficacy toward use of technology and the internet, but this is not reflected in superior performance and active involvement in online social interactions. Because female students have higher levels of academic self-efficacy, their overall performance in online courses tends to be slightly better than males

(Chang et al., 2014). Female online students tend to place a greater emphasis on relational and communication aspects of the online environment, particularly with instructors. This shows that male and female students may behave differently in several ways in online courses. It is important to recognize that most learners, women or men, are adaptable and cognitively flexible, especially if motivated.

Integrated Framework for Designing the Online Learning Experience

Our proposed framework comprises four interrelated learning dimensions: cognitive, emotional, behavioral, and social. The design of learner-centered learning experiences involves using these dimensions to guide the design of various aspects of the online course environment. The framework also identifies five design aspects of the learning environment that learners encounter and interact with in their journey through an online course. These aspects serve as focal points for instructors and course designers to enhance the learning experience. They include (a) course structure and interface, (b) content interactions, (c) learning activities, (d) social interactions, and (e) assessments and feedback. The design of each aspect is shaped by elements from each of the four dimensions. The aim is to provide instructors and course designers with a practical, holistic, and evidence-based framework for achieving learner-centered design goals. The skillful application of this framework can result in more meaningful, engaging, and deep learning experiences for online learners. Figure 2.2 shows the integrated framework for designing the online learning experience and how the four dimensions interact with the course design aspects.

Dimensions of the Learning Experience

The inner circle of the integrated framework depicts the interplay of the cognitive, emotional, behavioral, and social dimensions of learning that comprise the learning experience. These dimensions need to be approached both separately and as a unified whole. Each dimension comes into play in various degrees through learner interactions within the online environment as they encounter the five online course aspects. For example, when learners engage in certain learning activities involving group collaboration, the social dimension will assume primacy whereas the other three dimensions of learning remain active but to a lesser degree. Similarly, when learners are

Figure 2.2. Integrated framework for designing the online learning experience.

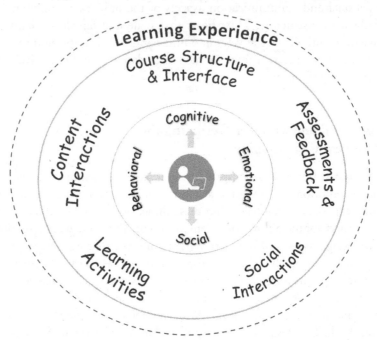

interacting with complex content, the cognitive dimension will dominate but could involve to a lesser extent the behavioral and social dimensions of learning. The emotional dimension often underlies and permeates just about every type of learning experience. The most impactful learning experiences are intentionally designed to integrate the four dimensions, in various combinations, in almost every aspect of the online learning experience. Let's examine each of these dimensions and their contributions to the learner experience. Note that the framework refers to a learning experience; courses comprise multiple interconnected learning experiences.

Cognitive Dimension

Bloom's taxonomy of learning objectives, developed in 1956, continues to be one of the most well-known and used frameworks for educators in designing learning programs and courses (Bloom & Krathwohl, 1956). The taxonomy is composed of three domains of learning: cognitive, affective, and psychomotor. The subject matter and learning objectives for most online courses focus primarily on the cognitive dimension. Incorporating the cognitive dimension into the learning experience design process involves understanding a few related concepts: deep learning and cognitive capacity.

Deep Learning

Online courses strive to engage learners on a cognitive level through various types of interaction with the course content, instructor, and other learners (Moore, 2013). A learner's invested cognitive effort when involved in these interactions significantly impacts learning outcomes. Two types of learning orientations related to cognition have been addressed in educational psychology: shallow learning and deep learning (Graesser et al., 2010). Shallow learning, often referred to as surface learning, involves memorization of new ideas, phrases, facts, and information. It results in minimal depth of conceptual understanding and cognitive processing. In contrast, deep learning occurs when learners fully exercise mental resources in order to comprehend complicated material, understand complex concepts, solve problems requiring analysis and synthesis, and make difficult decisions by drawing on discipline-specific knowledge and experience. According to Graesser and D'Mello (2011), "Deep learning occurs when there is a discrepancy between the task at hand and the person's prior knowledge and the discrepancy is identified and corrected" (p. 2). Their research also reveals that deep learning is often accompanied by discomfort, which when managed properly by instructors compels learners to exert more cognitive effort.

Cognitive Capacity

Learning is highly dependent on the cognitive processes learners bring to bear on a learning task. It requires an ability to select, organize, and connect new information with existing knowledge stored in long-term memory (Mayer et al., 2008). A major challenge for all learners stems from an inherent limited capacity of memory resources, particularly working memory. Working memory imposes a serious limitation on how much new information a person can take in and process before it can be assimilated and stored in long-term memory for later recall and use. Working memory is a precious cognitive resource that is highly susceptible to overload.

Cognitive overload typically occurs when learners are presented with large amounts of new content or required to study highly complex subject material (Sweller, 1994). Online courses that are content laden can be cognitively taxing and require specific design strategies to avoid overloading a learner's processing capacity. For example, Mayer et al. (2008) have found that conceptual understanding of complex material can be negatively impacted when too many details are presented during the initial stages of learning new content. To manage cognitive load, instructors should introduce complex material by first ensuring learners grasp the conceptual and qualitative aspects of the topic and then gradually scaffold details and quantitative information.

The online environment includes a number of features that may divert cognitive resources away from learning. These features include (a) an emphasis on text-based communication, requiring more time and effort to generate and comprehend content, (b) use of LMS with interfaces that impose a less than user-friendly structure for accomplishing tasks such as navigating the course and accessing content, and (c) course software tools requiring considerable cognitive overhead to learn and use. All combined, these technology-related factors in the online environment can increase the cognitive burden imposed on learners above and beyond simply assimilating critical course content.

Those aspiring to become skilled learning experience designers need to adopt a type of cognitive empathy with learners. This requires first a sensitivity to the cognitive processes and demands imposed on learners as they interact with course content, instructors, and other learners via technology. Second, instructors need to emphasize deep learning and manage cognitive load to prevent learners from becoming overwhelmed when presented with large amounts of new content or complex subject matter.

Emotional Dimension

There seems to be a widespread awakening to the once neglected emotional side of the human experience. Developers of various products and services are increasingly recognizing the importance of emotional design (Norman, 2004, 2016) to enhance the experience of users, customers, patients, and patrons.

For decades, the emotional dimension of learning has been largely ignored and rarely discussed by instructors and course designers in higher education. Yet research in the learning sciences has begun to confirm what many teachers have suspected—that most impactful and meaningful learning experiences are imbued with emotions. Research shows that deep learning cannot be achieved through cold cognition (independent of emotional involvement) and that most learning events involve an intricate interplay between cognition, affect, motivation, and social interaction (Graesser & D'Mello, 2011; Pekrun, 2011; Tyng et al., 2017).

Both positive and negative emotions can facilitate learning. Enjoyment and feeling good are not always positively correlated with deeper learning. Jackson and Graesser (2007) reported that students who are confronted with complex learning tasks often have the lowest ratings of enjoyment in conditions where they learned the most. Positive emotions such as delight seem to emerge after a period of at least moderate struggle when goals are met and problems are solved. The most profound learning activities involve just the right amount and type of challenge and deliberately designed confusion (D'Mello et al., 2014). Negatively charged emotions can be beneficial only to the extent that they promote deeper engagement with subject matter and can be managed and resolved successfully (Loderer et al., 2018). Online learners want their learning experiences to be enjoyable, engaging, and interesting; however, it is more difficult for instructors in a virtual setting to gauge the emotional climate of the course, to determine individual reactions to learning activities, and to rapidly detect when confusion might turn to frustration leading to a downward spiral of disengagement. There are three facets of the emotional dimension of learning in online course design that deserve attention: aesthetics, emotional presence, and motivation.

Aesthetics

Based on research into human–computer interaction (HCI) and affective computing, users respond at a visceral level to the aesthetic features of interface designs. Users tend to express greater satisfaction and higher levels of motivation in using applications that have aesthetically appealing interface features (Meyer, 2017). According to Norman (2004), "attractiveness produces positive emotions, causing mental processes to be more creative, more tolerant of minor difficulties" (p. 60). In their review of research on emotions in technology-based learning environments, Loderer et al. (2018) concluded that designing an aesthetically appealing online learning environment is an essential element of emotionally sound design. Learning environments that incorporate emotional elements through look, feel, and aesthetics can induce emotions that affect learner performance and cognitive processes including improved comprehension (Plass & Kaplan, 2016): "The effectiveness of instructional design will depend on the extent to which it takes into account the pervasive and motivating nature of emotions and their natural interconnections with cognition" (p. 134). Creating aesthetically pleasing course sites and learning materials is not just gratuitous fluff. It is an integral ingredient for accentuating natural human emotions that occur within almost all well-designed learning environments.

Emotional Presence

Cleveland-Innes and Campbell (2012) defined *emotional presence* as "the outward expression of emotion, affect, and feeling by individuals and among individuals in a community of inquiry, as they relate to and interact with the learning technology, course content, students, and the instructor" (p. 283). One way to convey a sense of emotional presence in online learning environments is through the use of personalized and conversational language in both instructional text and multimedia content. Mayer et al. (2004) showed the positive impact of incorporating emotional elements into learning materials through the use of the personalization principle. Infusing course content with a personal tone and feel can result in heightened levels of learner engagement, motivation, and improved learning outcomes (Reichelt et al., 2014). Also, the increased use of video by instructors, in the form of recorded video messages and live video conferencing, adds a new level of personal expression and emotional presence to online communications.

Motivation

There is a strong emotional undercurrent associated with motivation and learning. Instructors know the joy and gratification of working with highly motivated learners as well as the challenges and frustrations of working with less motivated individuals. Positive emotions such as excitement, interest, and confidence and negative emotions like frustration, confusion, and boredom often ebb and flow throughout an entire course. Such feelings influence a learner's invested mental effort, which is a reflection of their motivation or involvement in performing learning tasks (Paas et al., 2005). Even under optimal learning conditions, where instructors provide clearly written and well-organized content, deep learning will not occur without the internal condition of learner motivation (Bolkan et al., 2016).

In the online environment, learner motivation is much more difficult for instructors to monitor and influence than in a face-to-face classroom setting. In an online course, it is easier for learners to procrastinate and avoid in-depth interactions with subject material and members of the learning community. Michelle Miller (2014), a cognitive psychologist who teaches online, recommended in her book *Minds Online* that online instructors need to develop at least an informal game plan for motivating their learners. She advised that instructors and course designers "think like psychologists, getting into students' mental processes to figure out how to spark the forces that move them" (p. 167). Instructors need to devote more attention to the learners' emotional journey throughout an online course and incorporate motivational elements into each of the five aspects of course design.

Behavioral Dimension

The online learning environment evokes a variety of behaviors associated with learners' technology-mediated interactions with content, people, and course-related software. The behavioral dimension of learning focuses broadly on observable learner actions or what they "do" in the online environment. This dimension can be linked to certain mental activities that drive behaviors such as making decisions in interactive simulations, learning games, and scenarios. It encompasses performing tasks, practicing, exploring content, navigating the course website, and responding to people and situations in the virtual space. There are two aspects of the behavioral dimension from a learning experience design perspective that are important: learner interaction with technology and learner application of knowledge.

Learner Interaction With Technology
In the online environment, learners interact with technologies and tools within a digital learning ecosystem. Clicking objects on the screen, scrolling, eye focusing, and tasks performed related to accessing and interacting with content are just a few behavioral examples. HCI research has contributed to a better understanding of the human experience in various types of computer-based environments and how user interfaces can be designed to make frequently performed actions and tasks easier and more efficient (Norman, 2005; O'Brien & Lebow, 2013). In addition, work in the field of user experience design offers strategies applicable in designing learner-centered information architectures for online environments (Garrett, 2011). Design strategies from these related fields can be applied to almost every aspect of the online course space.

Learner Application of Knowledge
The behavioral dimension aligns with the practice of writing learning objectives in observable behavioral terms that focus on doing, producing, and demonstrating knowledge and skills—closing the gap between thinking and doing, knowing about and knowing how. Learners take newly acquired knowledge and apply it through learning activities involving choices, decisions, solutions, and artifacts as outcomes of what they can do with their newly acquired knowledge. Conversely, a "learning by doing" strategy can be used where learners acquire knowledge and skills as they perform challenging tasks. Online learning activities that emphasize the behavioral dimension often adopt active learning strategies used in many face-to-face and blended courses. Practice activities, interactive case scenarios, virtual laboratories, and games and simulations are all examples of how the behavioral dimension of learning can be accentuated to promote application of knowledge in the online environment.

Social Dimension

In the online environment, there is a need to adapt certain senses (e.g., vision, hearing, and touch) to connect with others and create a sense of closeness. For example, in the online environment we cannot touch objects or smell or taste food. There is a need to create a perceptual experience that happens at the cognitive, emotional, and behavioral levels. Mind, emotions, and behaviors come together in a dynamic interplay, creating the perceptual presence, a sensory experience of "being there" and "being together" with others (Lehman & Conceição, 2010, p. 7). This involves a *social experience of presence*, which Lehman and Conceição (2010) defined as having "a sense of being with others and responding to each other" (p. 16). The social dimension of learning involves two main types of social interactions: learner interactions with the instructor and learner interactions with other learners.

Learner Interactions With the Instructor

The quality of an online learner's interaction with the instructor has been found to be one of the most essential elements that determine a student's perception of learning in the online environment (Marks et al., 2005). Instructor–learner interactions help mitigate feelings of isolation and disconnection. Instructor presence can facilitate and model critical discourse and provide constructive feedback. Baker (2010) found a statistically significant positive relationship between instructor immediacy or responsiveness and perceived presence, particularly in courses that used synchronous interactions. Ladyshewsky's (2013) study showed how the role of the instructor can influence student satisfaction when social presence, driven by the instructor, appears to drive learning quality.

Part of learner experience design involves becoming aware of discrepancies between what instructors believe to be important to learners and what learners value most from their interactions with their online instructors. An accurate understanding of learner expectations and desires is an important factor in designing more satisfying and motivating social learning experiences. Dennen et al. (2007) discovered that many instructors orient their interactions with learners around course content and learners' ability to demonstrate their knowledge of course content. However, student data reveal other criteria that instructors should heed. These factors included (a) responding to learner-initiated communication in a timely manner, (b) demonstrating continuous presence in course discussion forums, and (c) explicitly stating expectations for discussion behaviors including examples and models. Skilled discussion facilitators also recognize that it is not the volume or amount of instructor communication that matters most but rather the frequency and quality of the content conveyed.

Learner Interactions With Other Learners

This social dimension has to do with how well learners participate in online learning mediated by technology and feel they are together with others. The learner experience from a social perspective is quite unique in the online space. Contrasted with a face-to-face environment, the online space "requires psychological, cognitive, and emotional connection to feel, think, and behave in a way that is appropriate for the online environment" (Lehman & Conceição, 2014, p. 17).

One important component of the social dimension in the online environment is relationship-building through the creation of a learning community. Garrison et al. (2003) developed the community of inquiry model, which involves three elements in the online learning experience: cognitive presence, social presence, and instructor presence. Cognitive presence is the ability to start, create, and validate meaning through reflection and dialogue with others. Social presence involves personal and emotional connection to the learning community. Social presence can promote cognitive presence through the expression of thoughts, ideas, and feelings as they relate to others while learning together. Instructor presence is the instructor's influence in initiating, facilitating, and monitoring learner interactions with other learners, which is key to enhancing the quality of the social dimension of the online learning experience.

Course Design Aspects

The integrated framework identifies five design aspects of the online learning environment that instructors and course designers can use as focal points in their efforts to enhance the learning experience. Online course learning experiences are shaped by the interplay of these five aspects supported by the four dimensions of learning. Figure 2.3 shows the five course design aspects. A brief description of each aspect is provided next.

Course Structure and Interface

This aspect is the medium through which course content and social interactions take place involving instructors and learners. This aspect has design features that are heavily influenced by the LMS. The online course structure refers to the organization of course-related content into units, lessons, modules, resources, and other digital learning materials. The learner interface is the visual medium between the learner and the technology-driven learning environment. The interface displays content through a variety of page layouts, each with a particular look and feel that also contain clickable items such as menus and navigational controls. These elements combine to form a cohesive whole, providing a stage upon which individuals interact with content and people in the virtual space.

Figure 2.3. Course design aspects.

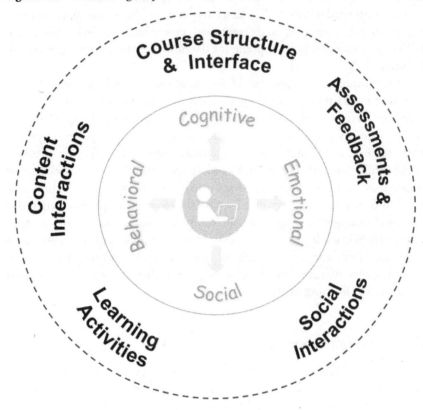

Content Interactions

This aspect pertains to the design of course content material specifically for instructional purposes. Much of it involves the work of an instructor creating, organizing, structuring, and presenting content both synchronously and asynchronously using various media and message design strategies. Content can be presented to learners in the form of written documents, online learning modules and tutorials, case studies, multimedia presentations, videos, podcasts, and synchronous presentations (webinars). Well-designed content interactions engage learners and, most importantly, promote deep learning.

Learning Activities

Using the integrated approach to online course design, conventional assignments can often be reframed and expanded into learning activities, where they take on a more comprehensive form as "learning experiences" in and of themselves. Learning activities can be designed to accomplish higher-level learning objectives involving analysis, application, synthesis, and evaluation, integrating a number of learning tasks. They can be purposefully and skillfully designed to actively engage learners at the cognitive, emotional, behavioral, and social dimensions of learning. By exploiting the potential of new digital pedagogies and technologies, online learning activities can incorporate optimal levels of challenge, contextualization (linkage to real-world situations), story and narrative, active learning, and learner agency and choice.

Social Interactions

The social interaction aspect of online course design includes technology-mediated interpersonal communications between individuals, groups, and instructors to facilitate learning. These include discussion forums, emails, instructor messaging, and chats that occur around and are related to formal course subject matter (content interactions). These interactions can provide instructor coaching, mentoring, and guidance while enhancing instructor–learner and learner–learner connections that promote engagement and deep learning. Instructor-managed social interactions involve design skills including the use of personalized communication and projection of copresence, intimacy, and immediacy.

Assessments and Feedback

Learning assessments are integral to the entire learning experience design process and are embedded within course content, learning activities, and social interactions. They are formative and run throughout the online course, providing detailed representations of learners' progress and achievement. Feedback constitutes any messages from an instructor, formal or informal, in response to a learner action (Mason & Bruning, 2001). How instructors design and provide feedback in an online setting impacts learner motivation and self-confidence—and learning outcomes.

Learning Experience Design Principles and Strategies

Learning experience design requires online instructors and course designers to cultivate a learner-centered mindset, always being sensitive to the cognitive, emotional, behavioral, and social learning needs of learners. We offer five core principles that guide design decisions for each of the design aspects in the integrated framework for designing the online learning experience. These principles are incorporated into the design strategies throughout this book. They should be in the foreground of the experience design process and help integrate the four learning dimensions and the five design aspects into a holistic experience.

Cognitive Design Principle: Design Learning Experiences for Cognitive Engagement

Designing learning experiences draws on evidence-based guidelines to understand how individuals process and assimilate new information and apply it to learning tasks. Learning experience design is also concerned with how learners leverage cognitive processing demands as they engage with different kinds of content and learning interactions. The following strategies can help promote cognitive development:

- Managing cognitive load in how complex content is designed and presented
- Accommodating certain learner characteristics related to the cognitive dimension of learning
- Selecting appropriate media formats that effectively make learning more efficient
- Creating intuitive interfaces, menus, and content structures
- Conducting social interactions that reinforce cognitive engagement
- Promoting learner–content and learner–instructor interactions that promote deep learning
- Providing assessments and feedback that cognitively challenge and stimulate learners

These strategies focus on crafting learning interactions in ways that help learners use their cognitive capacities efficiently and effectively to accomplish learning goals.

Emotional Design Principle: Design Learning Experiences for Emotional Connection

Designing impactful online learning experiences should incorporate affective elements to promote learner engagement and increase invested mental effort (Plass & Kaplan, 2016). Enhancing learner motivation increases engagement and activates cognitive processes that lead to deeper learning. Placing emotions and motivation in the foreground is one of the biggest shifts in the practice of learning experience design. Emotions are drivers of learning (Pekrun, 2011); cognitive and emotional elements are inextricably bound together in almost every learning experience. Learning experience design pays particular attention to affective elements that have been shown to positively impact learning and learner satisfaction. Strategies that evoke emotional connection include the following:

- Incorporating aesthetic and visually appealing features into the course interface
- Integrating motivational elements that arouse curiosity, challenge, and relevance
- Using a personalized communication style in content design and social discourse
- Writing learning objectives in ways that learners understand while sparking their interest
- Incorporating instructor feedback throughout the course to inspire, encourage, and motivate learners

These strategies focus on design efforts to activate and sustain learner interest and motivation to allow fuller engagement with every aspect of the online course experience.

Behavioral Design Principle: Design Learning Experiences That Connect Knowledge to Application

The quality of the knowledge learners construct at the cognitive level often remains unknown to the instructor and others in the online course environment. The gold standard for assessing learning outcomes is for learners to demonstrate what they can do or how they can apply their knowledge. This principle involves active learning and practice. Learners perform various tasks repeatedly, receiving corrective feedback until they achieve mastery. The following strategies can augment the behavioral dimension of online learning:

- Designing learner interfaces that permit easy navigation and access to course materials
- Crafting content that provides retrieval practice and scaffolding for supporting the performance of certain learning tasks
- Creating learning activities that involve active and generative learning tasks focused on application of higher-order knowledge and skills
- Integrating knowledge application and skills into social learning activities
- Embedding performance-type assessments, practice exercises, and game elements into learning activities

These strategies focus on bridging the cognitive, emotional, and social dimensions of learning with opportunities for learners to apply and practice what they have learned.

Social Design Principle: Design Learning Experiences That Support the Social Needs of Learners

Skillful design of online social interactions can alleviate the feelings of isolation and disconnection that the online environment may create due to the absence of physical presence. Designing online learning experiences that encourage copresence, intimacy, and immediacy activates the social and emotional dimensions of learning. Social interactions are the medium for keeping learners motivated and intellectually curious to learn. Strategies that support the social needs of learners include the following:

- Establishing a personalized, safe, and open social climate for intellectual conversations
- Creating an intuitive and personalized interface around virtual social interactions
- Connecting learners to content, instructor, and other learners through personalized communication
- Promoting deep learning through social engagement
- Sustaining and influencing learner motivation through instructor feedback and presence

These strategies focus on social interactions involving discourse between instructor and learner and among learners that build on cognitive, behavioral, and emotional dimensions.

Integration Design Principle: Design Learning Experiences by Integrating the Four Learning Dimensions

There is a tendency in many online courses for content elements, learning activities, assessments, and social interactions to appear fragmented and disconnected from each other. This fragmentation is apparent in the way online courses present lists of loosely connected content and tasks. Learning experience design emphasizes a more holistic design where content units, learning activities, social interactions, and assessments are more closely interconnected and learning goals are made more transparent to the learner. Strategies for creating holistic learning experiences include the following:

- Using pedagogical wrappers around content units, learning activities, social interactions, and assessments to make explicit their relevance and interconnection
- Interweaving the four dimensions of learning into the design of content units, learning activities, social interactions, and assessments

- Incorporating content that integrates multiple media formats and learning strategies
- Integrating social interactions with content modules and reading assignments

These strategies focus on thinking holistically about the design of learning experiences.

Implementing the Framework for Designing the Online Learning Experience

We cannot emphasize enough that learner empathy is the foundation of learner experience design. It is best achieved by the instructor or course designer taking on the perspective of the learner and addressing design deficiencies through talking and listening to learners and understanding their characteristics and needs. Learners respond positively to experiences that bring satisfaction and relevance to their work and life. Making course content relevant to learners' personal goals through manageable, meaningful, and active learning activities can create engaging and deep learning experiences. Focusing design efforts on the structural framework and learner interface, content interactions, learning activities, social interactions, and assessments and feedback can create a space that stimulates the active construction and application of knowledge. Underlying and supporting these design aspects are four learning dimensions (cognitive, emotional, behavioral, and social). These dimensions are interrelated as they build on each other to increase frequency and duration of flow experiences throughout an online course. The following five chapters will focus on each design aspect and strategies for creating a holistic learning experience.

The integrated framework is intended to help instructors and course designers make the shift from conventional content-focused course designs to a learner-centered design. One key pedagogical goal of learning experience design is to promote learner engagement and deep learning. For those interested in updating or revising an existing online course, we recommend identifying one or two course aspects most in need of improvement based on learner feedback. It is always best to use learner feedback in identifying where design deficiencies exist. For those developing new online courses or converting a face-to-face course to the online environment, we recommend focusing on each course design aspect in the order that best suits the course project management process.

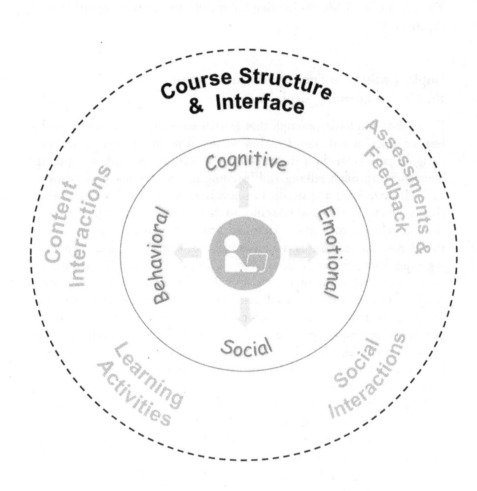

3

DESIGNING THE COURSE
STRUCTURE AND
LEARNER INTERFACE

The first design aspect in the integrated framework for designing the online learning experience focuses on the content structure and the graphical interface of the online learning space. This aspect constitutes the medium or stage within which all learner interactions in the online learning environment occur. The design of this aspect is often transparent to learners, yet it influences the learning experience in multiple ways related to the cognitive, emotional, and behavioral dimensions of learning.

After the course learning objectives and content scope have been determined, instructors and course designers concentrate on how course content units will be structured and presented in an easy, understandable, and appealing way to the learner. Throughout this chapter we will use concepts and principles from the field of UXD and adapt them in the design of the online learning space. We will look first at what is involved in designing a structural framework to support the primary learning goals of a course. After considering common challenges and scenarios involved in designing a course structure, we shift focus to the design of the learner interface and its impact on the learning experience. We conclude the chapter by presenting strategies for designing the online learning environment, applying design thinking and learner-centered design principles.

Guiding Design Questions

- How can we use a course conceptual model to shape and focus the design of the course structure to better accomplish learning goals and meet learner needs?

- How can we design a course structure that is meaningful to learners and organized to better support specific kinds of learning outcomes?
- How can we apply design thinking and UXD to create a learner-centered online course interface?

From Conceptual Model to Course Structure

As in all human design endeavors, the creation of an online course begins with a conceptual model. Understanding the conceptual model underlying a course and creating a structural framework is the starting point for all course design projects. In this section, we explain how a conceptual model for an online course gives purpose and shape to the course content structure. We will also look at common design challenges and scenarios related to creating the online course structure.

Course Conceptual Models

A conceptual model is a mental image (representation) in the mind of a course creator that serves as a kind of matrix, giving rise to the design of the course content structure and shaping other aspects of the online course environment. The conceptual model envisions certain global attributes of the course that include purpose and main learning goal, what it will do for learners, the form it will take, and how it will look and function.

The conceptual model specifies the course format—if the course will be instructor-led, self-paced, synchronous or asynchronous; the length of the course and timetable structure; and if it is credit or noncredit. For an online course, the conceptual model usually includes ideas about the technology delivery platform, including any LMS and what the course might look like and how it will function. In some cases, it may also allude to preferred instructional methodologies that will be used, such as case study, project, lecture, or simulation approaches.

A not so tangible but probably the most important part of a course conceptual model that directly influences the design of the course structure lies in the primary purpose and learning goal for the course. There are two fundamental types (or categories) of courses based on their primary purpose and instructional goal (Romiszowski, 1981). For the first type of course, the main instructional goal is to acquaint learners with the core knowledge, vocabulary, principles, and structure of a domain or field of study. This type of course is most common in higher education, particularly at the undergraduate level. The structure of this type of course is typically organized around major topics related to the discipline. This contrasts with the second type of course, in which the primary goal and purpose is aimed at supporting learners in developing competencies and higher order, complex skills, often related to some aspect of a job or professional practice in the real world. This second type of course is common in many graduate and professional schools, certificate programs, and workforce training courses. The content structure of this type of course is typically organized around core tasks that support the acquisition of complex skills.

Most important about this distinction is that each type of course requires a different design for its structural framework. Although many courses ask learners to acquire both knowledge and skills, the primary purpose and learning goal of a course will tend toward one or the other. Courses designed around subject matter and domain knowledge place greater emphasis on "knowing about." Courses that focus on skill and performance competencies emphasize "knowing how." As we will see, these orientations influence the design of the course structure and other aspects of a course.

Course Structural Framework

Every course has a structure that holds together all content elements into a unified whole. Most instructors have experience designing a course structure and have a fair degree of latitude in how they do it. Creating a course structure involves first defining the content scope of the course based on learning objectives. Referring to course objectives, instructors identify major thematic units and organize the flow of course content into a logical sequence. Structuring content continues within each unit to the lesson or module level by identifying topics and subtopics.

Designing the structural framework for an online course requires going back to its conceptual model and focusing on the primary purpose of the course. If a course is aimed at having learners attain subject matter mastery in a domain, then the top-level thematic units comprising the course should concentrate mainly on major topics that constitute the subject domain. Topics are determined by the instructor's understanding of how knowledge is organized within the discipline. This topical structure is typically framed around key concepts, principles, and processes within the discipline. Developing competencies in performing tasks related to jobs becomes secondary to the acquisition of discipline-specific knowledge. Task-focused modules are generally in the form of learning activities, labs, projects, and other learning exercises that serve to reinforce knowledge construction.

Courses where the primary goal is acquiring complex skills and competencies and performing job-like tasks related to real-life contexts require a different type of content structure. In this case, the top-level thematic units are typically designed around core tasks that support a whole skill. The thematic units will also reflect the sequence of these skill sets based on how expert performers approach the skill as part of a job.

From a learning experience design perspective, a knowledge-topic focused course and a skill-task focused course can promote engagement and deep learning, but for two different purposes. For example, the structural framework of a course in financial planning could be organized in several ways. A course structure could be organized around discipline-specific knowledge that includes topics focusing on key concepts, principles, theories, and models used by expert financial planners. The same course could have a different structural framework organized around the job or skill sets of financial planning. In this instance, the thematic units would center on key tasks and subskills supporting the practice of financial planning. Subunits or lessons might include how to manage cash and credit or how to manage risk and investment strategies, along with task-based practice modules.

In designing the learner experience, instructors and course designers need to continually keep in mind alignment between their course's underlying conceptual models and its structural framework. Many online course descriptions claim to teach skills and application but are structured mostly around concepts and principles associated with a skill and only lightly focus on task performance that supports the skill. Learners are likely to experience disappointment when a course description based on its conceptual model is misaligned with its content structure.

Online Course Structure Design Challenges and Scenarios

The underlying conceptual model of most online courses has tended to mirror that of conventional face-to-face classroom-based instruction. In the course virtual space, face-to-face lectures become recorded PowerPoint videos, print-based readings become electronic texts, and group discussions become electronic discussion forums. Many online courses focus on teaching domain knowledge and are timetable-based with content broken down into units organized around lists of topics and subtopics. Not long ago the majority of online courses resembled organized content repositories where learners downloaded and absorbed information related to a subject and then discussed what they read in threaded discussion forums. These types of content-centric designs are now fading but still linger. Breaking from these entrenched traditional course design patterns is not easy. Designing learning experiences in a digital learning ecosystem entails taking advantage of new digital tools and pedagogies and using design thinking to shift the focus of online course content structures from information-centric to more learner-centric. In the following, we describe challenges instructors often encounter in making the shift to online.

Learning Management Systems and Institutional Juggernauts
Most LMSs have been designed to accommodate online courses that build on traditional conceptual models. One way they do this is by providing limited and one-size-fits-all templates for creating a course structural framework. In many ways, they reinforce the tendency to digitize existing course content and simply make it available to students to access online. Coates et al. (2005) stated that the built-in functions of the LMS can be a reinforcement of teaching as the "transmission of decontextuali[z]ed and discrete pieces of information" (p. 27), due to its text-heavy and linear nature. The kind of learning experiences the LMS fosters is restrictive because the learning activities tend to be organized based on uniform templates. The design of an online course structural framework can become especially challenging when an innovative instructor or course designer has a different conceptual model for an online course and would like to try something new that deviates from the templatized LMS-imposed structural framework. Innovative conceptual models may also run headlong into constraints imposed by existing institutional processes for online course development. These often go hand-in-hand with the LMS, emphasizing course production efficiency over the learner experience. Learning experience design often involves pushing the envelope, finding creative ways of working within the constraints of an LMS and institutional processes.

Converting a Face-To-Face Course to Online
In this situation, there is ample opportunity for instructors to give pause and defer the urge to plunge headlong into replicating an existing classroom-based conceptual model and course structure. Instead they can engage in design thinking by getting ideas from others and explore alternative structural frameworks. This may involve gaining a deeper understanding about learners, challenging assumptions about teaching and learning in an online environment, and brainstorming creative solutions. For example, a professor in the process of moving an existing French and Italian Renaissance literature course to the online environment brainstormed with colleagues and course designers about alternative ways to structure the course. Instead of organizing course units around a list of literary genres, he restructured the course units and lessons around various time periods and locations in Renaissance France and Italy. This shift in the course structural framework not only provided a real-world context for unit content but also opened the door for more creative ways to design lessons using a time travel theme. There are numerous

ways to restructure and reframe existing classroom-based content structures to make them more engaging for online learners. When making the shift from a face-to-face to an online course, one design thinking strategy is to regard the classroom course as a good working prototype. This involves first reflecting on course evaluations and feedback from students and identifying what was working and not working and then using this information to rethink how the learning experience could be made better when shifting to a new technology-enabled environment.

Designing a New Online Course
This situation broadens all the opportunities described previously for creating newer and better kinds of learner experience starting from the ground up and taking full advantage of using newer digital pedagogies. A worthy task for instructors and course designers creating new online courses from scratch is to rethink and push the envelope on conventional conceptual models and course structures for online courses. This may be a time to consider course designs that are more task- and competency-focused, that engage learners in more than just acquiring domain-specific knowledge, and incorporate more knowledge application opportunities related to performing practical real-world tasks. It is a good idea for instructors building new online courses to spend some time looking at a variety of examples of different online courses and focusing on their conceptual models and structural frameworks for inspiration. Becoming well acquainted with the design thinking process, the affordances of available technology tools, and collaborating with others are absolutely essential in this type of scenario and often lead to significant pedagogical innovations.

Making Changes to an Existing Online Course
For instructors and course designers with existing online courses, trying to make structural changes can easily become frustrating and a design mess where nothing seems to integrate. In this scenario, the most important thing may be to recognize the existing course conceptual model and structural framework that a course is based on and work as well as possible within the constraints. The best strategy here is to focus on making minor adjustments to the surface layer of the course structure, such as making unit and lesson titles more clear, interesting, and understandable from a learner perspective. The process should involve drawing upon learner feedback from previous instances of the course. Instructors can also identify smaller parts of the course within lessons for making enhancements. These are often not as tightly embedded into the existing course structure and might include new types of learning activities and links to content modules that reside outside

the course. Over time one can continue to make these minor enhancements, and their cumulative effect will result in significant improvements in the learner experience.

As we move into the next section, it becomes clearer how designing learning experiences is a holistic endeavor, as conceptual models, structural frameworks, and learner interface designs interrelate and impact the quality of the online learning experience.

The Learner Interface

The learner interface is the visual medium between the learner and the technology-driven learning environment. It is shaped by the underlying conceptual model and makes the structural framework of course content units visually explicit to learners.

Design Qualities of the Learner Interface

The design of the interface can enable or constrain the quality of interactions the learner has with content, instructors, and other learners. In observing learner interactions with electronic texts, Swan et al. (1998) found that the various structural features of e-text interfaces affected the meanings learners developed from the content. In addition, Swan et al. (2000) concluded that attributes of an online course's interface design such as consistency, clarity, transparency, and simplicity of course structures increased student perception of learning. These studies show that well-designed interfaces can better support learning and enhance the learning experience.

If an online course interface is overloaded with too many extraneous features and content elements, the learning space can be perceived as less useful and become overwhelming for learners. A learning space with a confusing and difficult-to-understand interface will not be used effectively and efficiently by learners and can negatively impact learning outcomes and the overall learning experience. The learner should be able to enter the online course environment and start using it immediately with little or no guidance. Norman (1990) has noted that the best designed interfaces are the ones that are hardly noticed, that permit the learner to focus on information and tasks rather than the mechanisms used to present the information and perform the task.

Effective learner interface design uses the principles of predictability, consistency, and content formatting. The visual layout of screens should be consistent with the mental models of the learner for how an online course should look and work. Predictability means the learner can accurately predict the outcome of interactions in the learning space. Before clicking on an object, the learner has a sense of what will happen. Consistency involves similar unit and lesson structures throughout the course represented in similar ways. Content formatting is when content is logically grouped together visually. These three principles help make the online learning experience intuitive and understandable.

Function of the Learner Interface

In the absence of a physical instructor, the online environment depends on a well-designed interface to help guide learners through their learning experience in the course (Lohr, 2000). The learner interface mediates the learner's interaction with course content, the instructor, and other learners. In the fields of HCI and UXD, this is often referred to as the *user interface*. There can be multiple levels of interfaces within any online learning environment comprising the course home page, menu structures for lessons, learning activities, discussion forums, and support resources. For online courses, the thematic units and lesson structure will stand out clearly in the main menu of the learner interface for easy access by students.

In the online environment, instructors and course designers need to become aware of the elements of effective learner interface design to provide a positive learning experience. The goals of interface design are to (a) provide learners with easy access to the information they need to achieve their goals (information architecture); (b) present information in a clear, organized, and easily understandable way (information design); and (c) offer a simple and elegant interface with an appealing look and feel (visual design). Achieving these goals sets the stage for positive learning experiences to occur as learners engage with the other four aspects of the online environment (content interactions, learning activities, social interactions, and assessment and feedback).

Information Architecture

The information architecture builds on the course structural framework. It involves mapping, organizing, and grouping categories of content in order to give the learner a sense of the scope and sequence of the course content. This is especially important for making clear the interrelationships between major content units and secondary-level lesson organization. Although it is not directly visible in the learner interface, the information architecture serves as a basis for developing menu structures for units, learning resources, lessons, and topics. Many course designs are based on bodies of organized knowledge within a discipline that learners need to access to complete assignments. A common information architecture for online courses is hierarchical and sequential. Many course content units and topics are organized around the weeks in a semester. This takes the form of content unit menus that resemble a text outline of topics based around dates. This architecture may be effective for representing, breaking down, and organizing a large body of content for easy access. However, from a learner perspective, it can often appear like a disconnected list of topics to get through and check off, fostering a learning process focused on rote content memorization.

The information architecture is represented through the learner interface and can serve a dual purpose. It can provide not only a visual topical structure but also a meaningful framework for learners to form an internal representation of the flow of the course content units, making the learner's journey through the course content more meaningful, application-focused, and motivating. Figure 3.1 shows a design of the main menu for an online

Figure 3.1. Main menu for an online course in consumer finance.

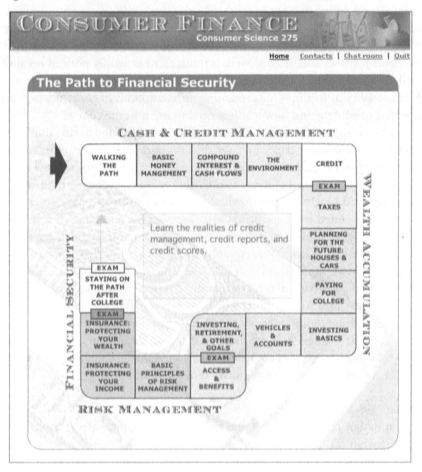

course in consumer finance. Notice how the course content is structured around a process involving four phases (Cash & Credit Management, Wealth Accumulation, Risk Management, and Financial Security). The course structural framework is based on a process using the analogy of a "path." As learners move through the course, which is based on a game board design, the underlying conceptual model, structural framework, information architecture, and interface design are tightly integrated, providing a more meaningful main menu screen.

From an information architecture perspective, learner-centered design involves understanding how course content can be visually structured, often in creative ways, so learners can access, absorb, process, and derive meaning from it.

Information Design

Information design occurs at a more granular level and focuses on communicating and presenting content so learners can understand information more easily and use it to perform tasks. Good information design ties content elements together and, if done well, is transparent or hardly noticed because well-designed content makes sense. It also involves selecting and using the best modality or medium for presenting different kinds of content based on the type of content and how learners need to use it in the course.

Several approaches can be used to improve the understandability of online course content pages in ways that support the cognitive dimension of learning and create more satisfying learner–content interactions. Horn's (1998a, 1998b) method of structured writing encourages the use of information maps and blocks as a way to visually organize informational elements of a topic. Structured writing distinguishes between flat and blocked text. Flat text, often referred to as a "wall of words" and common in much academic writing, consists of lengthy paragraphs that are not visually organized in a way that readers can see from its surface the structure of its contents. Blocked text makes the structure of text content more explicit through chunking large bodies of text into smaller units which are labeled. Blocked text is easier to comprehend and to find specific information in a document and is presented in a way that learners become more inclined to read. Figure 3.2 illustrates how blocking of text content and visual layout of screen content can enhance the learner experience at the cognitive dimension of learning.

Visual Design

Visual design refers to the graphic treatment of interface elements encompassing what the learner sees and interacts with in the online learning space. This includes the look and feel of text, images, and media objects on every

Figure 3.2. Information design of the learner interface.

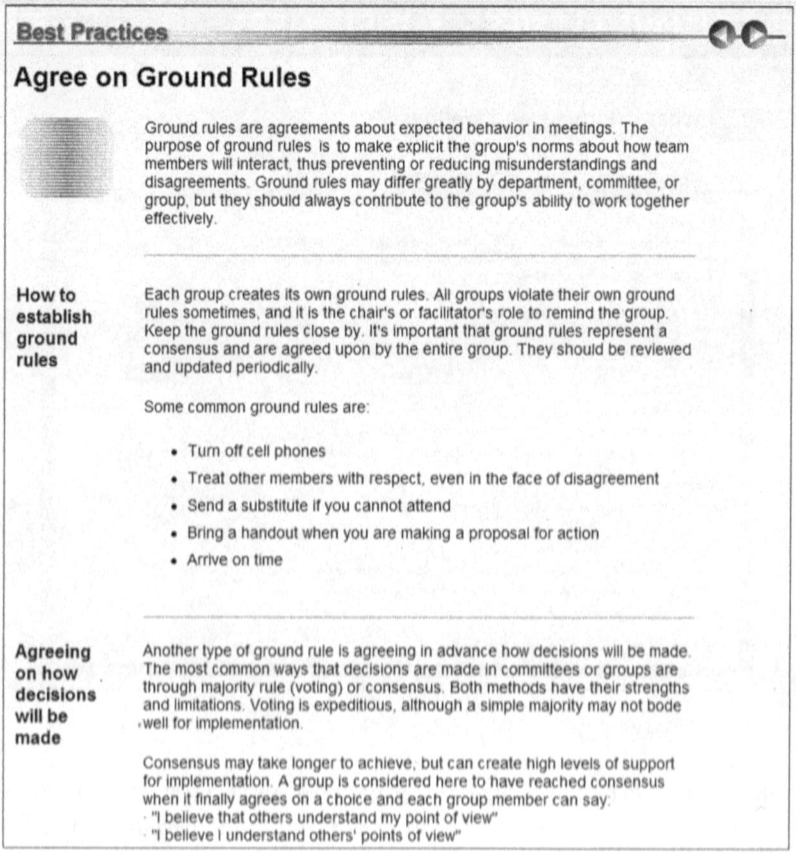

Best Practices

Agree on Ground Rules

Ground rules are agreements about expected behavior in meetings. The purpose of ground rules is to make explicit the group's norms about how team members will interact, thus preventing or reducing misunderstandings and disagreements. Ground rules may differ greatly by department, committee, or group, but they should always contribute to the group's ability to work together effectively.

How to establish ground rules

Each group creates its own ground rules. All groups violate their own ground rules sometimes, and it is the chair's or facilitator's role to remind the group. Keep the ground rules close by. It's important that ground rules represent a consensus and are agreed upon by the entire group. They should be reviewed and updated periodically.

Some common ground rules are:

- Turn off cell phones
- Treat other members with respect, even in the face of disagreement
- Send a substitute if you cannot attend
- Bring a handout when you are making a proposal for action
- Arrive on time

Agreeing on how decisions will be made

Another type of ground rule is agreeing in advance how decisions will be made. The most common ways that decisions are made in committees or groups are through majority rule (voting) or consensus. Both methods have their strengths and limitations. Voting is expeditious, although a simple majority may not bode well for implementation.

Consensus may take longer to achieve, but can create high levels of support for implementation. A group is considered here to have reached consensus when it finally agrees on a choice and each group member can say:
- "I believe that others understand my point of view"
- "I believe I understand others' points of view"

screen. All visual content has shape, line, color, spatial composition, and form and is part of the visual design. The visual design of the learning space is a layer that is built on top of the information architecture and information design, which initially are devoid of color and visual aesthetics. The look and feel of how informational and navigational elements are rendered and arranged on the screen can impact the learner experience on the cognitive, behavioral, and emotional levels.

The aesthetics (or visual appeal) of a course can influence how learners will judge their experience and enjoyment throughout the course (Lindgaard et al., 2006). The first intuitive reaction to the online course design affects how learners perceive relevance, trustworthiness, and value (Fessenden, 2017). Therefore, a positive first impression of the course site based on the design layout, color, content prioritization, and so on can set the tone for the

Figure 3.3. Visual look and feel of the learner interface.

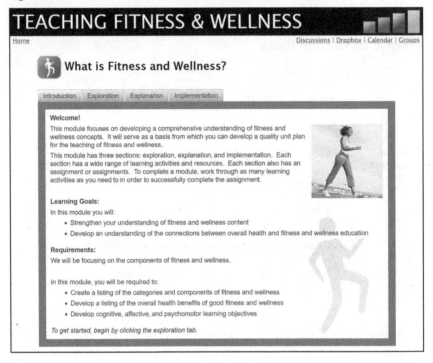

entire learning experience. Figure 3.3 provides an example of a visual look and feel of a learner interface. It embodies a simple and elegant design.

The look and feel of the online course can bring content, functionality, and aesthetics together, contributing to learner satisfaction and the overall learning experience. When designing an online course, it is essential to consider the emotional experiences of the learners (McEvoy & Cowan, 2016). Incorporating emotions into the course design requires empathy for the learner to intentionally create an experience that activates an emotional response.

Kahneman (2015) stated that there are two systems in which individuals process information. System 1 is the automatic system. This system is involuntary and involves little effort, but senses simple relationships or identifies patterns. System 2 requires attention and involves consciousness, awareness, and control. In System 1, the learner assesses the relevance of the course, quickly scans for significant course content, and tends to prioritize course aspects judged to be of high importance. Therefore, first impressions about the online course through the course interface can set the stage for the entire course.

The interface of the course can anticipate learner needs and guide the learner toward desirable learning. It is in System 1 that the learner perceives the aesthetics and the value of the course site (Kahneman, 2015). If the course site is aesthetically pleasing, the learner will feel like returning to the course and appreciating the learning activities. A course site that has poor visual design—no colors, too many different fonts, lack of contrast, and competing or extraneous graphics—may overwhelm the learner and undermine relevant course content and activities. Being sensitive to the design of the look and feel of the learner interface can serve to enhance the online learning space in a way that is attractive and appealing for the learner.

Interface Design Factors Influencing Learner Satisfaction

Chang and Tung (2008) stated that perception of usefulness, quality design, and ease of use are factors influencing online learner motivation (or behavioral intention) to use the online learning space. When learners enter and begin using the online learning space, they make tacit or implicit judgments regarding each of these factors contributing to their overall experience. The interface design needs to convey quality. The content needs to be framed and organized in ways that appear relevant and useful to learners. The potential constellation of interactions embodied in the learner interface needs to be user-friendly and simple to use.

Perceived usefulness and ease of use of the online learning environment lead to greater learner satisfaction with the learning experience, which contributes to increased persistence. Joo et al. (2011) found that perceived usefulness and ease of use impacted learner satisfaction more so than elements of social presence. This underscores the importance of a learner-friendly interface design and a structural framework that clearly communicates the relevance and practicality of the course content.

Learner interactions with the course interface impact their perception of the functionality, usefulness, and the ease of use of the online learning space, all of which impact motivation for continued participation in the online learning experience. Cho et al. (2009) stated that learner interface design is one of the most important aspects impacting the learning experience. Interface design comes into play at the course, lesson, and learning activity levels in online courses.

In the eyes of the learner, the interface is the face of the learning space. Ideally, it works on all four dimensions of learning to create a learner-centered experience. At the cognitive level, the learner can get a sense of the structure, flow, and form of the course content. It presents content in a concrete visual way, so that the learner can interact with and move through the learning space. At the cognitive and behavioral levels, the interface provides learners with the right amount of relevant content at the right times through the course to accomplish tasks. At the emotional level, the interface shows value in the learner's mind early on and throughout the course. The learner can see content flows and progress forward to achieve course goals and become more motivated to engage in learning activities. At the social level, the interface provides a personalized look and feel and a sense of presence such that the individual does not feel isolated and alone.

Aesthetics play an important role when designing the look and feel of the online learning environment. Tractinsky et al. (2000) concluded that the perceived beauty of a software product increased positive perceptions of its usability in their study. Thus, what is designed well in terms of usability and practicality will be perceived as attractive and desirable (Hassenzahl, 2004; Tuch et al., 2012).

It is important to have a balanced design strategy for the look and feel of online learning spaces that adheres to a "simple and elegant" design principle. This takes into consideration what Lavie and Tractinsky (2004) called the classical aesthetics dimension, which "emphasize[s] orderly and clear design and [is] closely related to many of the design rules advocated by usability experts" (p. 269). These considerations guide the design decisions around look and feel.

Strategies for Creating an Online Course Structure and Learner Interface

Design thinking is used in creating both the course structure and interface from a learner perspective. It is a creative and iterative process that often begins with initial and sometimes fuzzy ideas that get refined over time. We offer several design thinking strategies beginning with designing the course structure followed by strategies for designing the learner interface. But first you need to determine the primary goal and purpose of the course based on the conceptual framework.

Determine Primary Goal and Purpose of the Course Based on the Conceptual Model

The course conceptual model shapes the structural framework for the online course, which in turn shapes content elements of the learner interface. If the primary aim of a course is to have learners acquire knowledge of a domain or academic subject area, then the course content structure can be organized around thematic units corresponding to major topics within the discipline (i.e., concepts, principles, processes). If the primary aim of a course is to have learners acquire skills and competencies for performing complex tasks, such as those related to a profession, then it is often best to organize the content structure around thematic units that reflect constituent subtasks (i.e., smaller

TABLE 3.1
Aligning Course Goal/Purpose With Thematic Unit Structure

If primary course purpose/goal is:	*Then use this type of thematic unit:*
Knowledge of domain subject matter for a discipline of study	Major **topics** focusing on key concepts, principles, structures, or processes within the discipline
Performance of skills and complex tasks related to aspects of a job or profession	Core constituent **tasks** supporting the performance of a whole skill or complex task (part of a job or larger skill set)

skill sets related to performing more complex operations). Table 3.1 provides a simple heuristic for aligning a course's primary learning goal, expressed in the conceptual model, with the design of its structural framework.

Design a Meaningful and Organized Course Structure for Learning

Well-designed courses make their structural framework explicit to learners by organizing the course content into major thematic units that follow a logical sequence and where the interrelationships of units are made clear (Fink, 2013). Although there is no one best way to create an online course structure, we offer four strategies that apply design thinking to make the course structure more understandable and meaningful for learners and, just as important, more tightly focused on course learning goals.

Focus on Core Topics or Tasks

The starting point or foundation for building course content structurally aligned with the course's primary purpose and goal is to begin listing and sequencing the major thematic units based on the primary course goal. This can take the form of a simple skeletal outline on paper or a whiteboard.

Because design thinking is an iterative process, the initial list of thematic units should be regarded as a first draft. This high-level scope and sequence might include from seven to nine thematic unit titles, depending on the scope and length of the course. From here, instructors can begin to flesh out titles for subunit topics or tasks at the lesson or module level. The focus is on the big picture, not getting mired in content details. It is like zooming out with a camera and focusing on the structure of an object. The key is to sequence or arrange units so they clearly build on one another in a way such that learners would be able to integrate topics and tasks with preceding ones as the course unfolds. Topics can be sequenced based on chronology, simple to complex, or fundamental topics to more complex ones (Fink, 2013). van Merriënboer and Kirschner (2018) proposed a model for teaching complex skills and tasks in which a task unit's lesson structure consisted of (a) supportive information that explains how to approach problems and tasks in a skill domain, (b) procedural information that specifies how to perform routine aspects of a task, and (c) whole-task and part-task practice exercises.

Get Feedback and Refine

One key principle to learner-centered design using design thinking is to avoid coming to closure too quickly with initial ideas. A first draft course structural framework is only a starting point in need of refinement and will benefit from input from others. Being open to exploring alternative ways to structure and title course content units in ways that are meaningful and make sense for learners is key to a course design that is learner-focused from the top down. To aid in adopting a learner perspective, good instructors and course designers often sketch out on a whiteboard or flip chart the major unit, topic, and module content structure as if they were menu items within a course interface. The idea is to step back and consider how a learner might think and feel coming into the course and viewing the flow of unit thematic titles and underlying module subtopics. Learner-centered design is participatory, and getting feedback and ideas from not only colleagues but also several learners can only make it better. Because these are very rough skeletal sketches, it is easy to cross out items, rename them, and draw arrows to move items around. This entire process can be done rapidly, probably in less than an hour.

Explore Different Organizational Strategies

The course thematic units will reflect the most important topics and tasks experts in a domain feel are most important or fundamental for achieving a course's primary learning goals. Instructors or course designers should always consider alternative ways to structure course units, subunits, lessons, and modules using the design thinking strategy of brainstorming to explore and refine initial ideas. For example, alternative course structural frameworks might be built around a step-by-step process so that by the end of a course learners will know how to do something or create a product. Unit and lesson structures could incorporate sets of principles that experts in a discipline follow. Other approaches might involve having lesson content modules revolve around a series of case studies or scenarios where learners practice making decisions as an expert might do in real-world settings. As instructors or course designers continue iterating and refining the top-level course structure, framework ideas will emerge about how lessons and modules could be designed or structured. These ideas should all be captured and refined at the appropriate time.

Avoid Fragmentation

In designing course content structures attention should be given to avoiding fragmentation, whereby units and lessons seem disconnected and learners lose a sense of cohesiveness and interrelationships of the parts to the whole. Integration occurs when top-level thematic units not only have flow and cohesiveness but also include connections to the whole skill or knowledge domain when learners are engaged in lesson unit content. To prevent this sense of fragmentation, it is often a good idea to have the first unit of the course provide an overview of the whole course subject or skill performance to show how the parts (units, lessons) interrelate and integrate. Also, the course structure should include units or lessons devoted to whole-topic and whole-task integration.

Developing a learner-centered course structure from the ground up lays a foundation for starting the design of the online course learner interface.

Design a Simple, Usable, and Appealing Learner Interface

The learner interface is a learner-facing layer that makes visible the course structural framework and information architecture. It involves the design of screen layouts, the way information is presented, and the look and feel of the entire course site. For many instructors, much of the learner interface design is provided by the LMS, for better or worse. Instructors and course designers will need to work with the tools and templates provided with their particular LMS, which may consist of fairly limited interface design options. With this in mind, we provide several strategies from the field of UXD that incorporate design thinking practices into the interface design process. Readers, particularly those constrained by an LMS, are recommended to adapt and incorporate elements of these strategies into their interface design process wherever possible.

Build on the Information Architecture

Before beginning work on the learner interface, the course information architecture with its underlying structural framework must be fleshed out at the course unit and lesson topic levels. This could be in the form of a skeletal outline or even a rough sketch of how the course units and lessons might be visually structured. It is also a good idea to have at least one lesson-level content structure mapped out that represents how most lessons in the course will be structured and organized. A sample lesson should also include example content elements such as lesson introductory material, prototype media material, worksheets, and other major lesson elements that occur in other lessons. The online course environment will also contain other components, not directly related to course instructional content, that will also need to be accessed by students frequently in the interface. These are usually linked to from the course homepage and often provided by the LMS. These might include links to the course syllabus; a list of members of the course community; a course announcement panel; and links to resources, grades, and other common online course services. A list of all these components is needed to start the interface design process. In cases where a course website already exists to be redesigned, all of these components can be identified on the existing site. Also, in the case of redesigning an existing course interface, it is useful to view the current design as a prototype.

Start With Sketches

Learner interface design begins by sketching out ideas on paper or a whiteboard of what the ideal interface for a particular course will look like and how it might function. These sketches have often been referred to as storyboards or mockups. Most course designers now refer to them as *wireframes* (Garrett, 2011). Wireframes are used to envision preliminary screen designs in order to (a) visualize the layout of screens for the course homepage, unit and lesson menus, lesson activity pages, and other content-related pages; (b) envision and refine the design of screens that include combinations of text, graphics, audio, and video content; and (c) show how navigation between various sections of the course environment will work.

Wireframes are rough sketches used to work through design ideas and are not concerned with colors, fonts, specific images, or look and feel. The goal is to iterate and explore ideas of how the course content structure and other components will be presented from the outside in, or how the learner will see and interact with them. Even if there is an existing online course to be redesigned, wireframes can be used to represent the desired types of changes to be made. Figure 3.4 shows an example of an early wireframe sketch for the interface design of the consumer finance course depicting the top-level course structure lesson level. These are created very quickly and discarded for new ones when design changes are proposed.

Using wireframes helps to keep the learner perspective in the forefront of the designer's mind at all levels of the course. By having sketches of ideal learner-centered interfaces for different parts of the course, LMS templates often can be tweaked or workarounds can be developed to at least get closer to the ideal design depicted in a wireframe.

Get Early Feedback and Revise

The main purpose for creating wireframes is to get early feedback from others regarding the vision for an online course environment. This is similar to what an architect does when they show clients a blueprint of what a building structure will look like and how it will function before it is built. These prototype designs will need to meet the needs of both students and instructors, so it is important that they be shown to students who will be taking

Figure 3.4. Course and lesson levels wireframe.

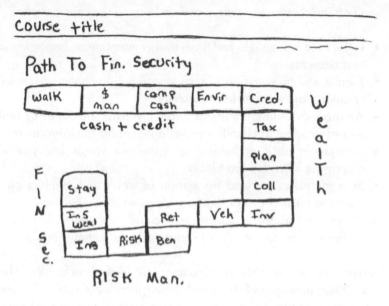

or have previously taken the course to get their feedback and ideas. The wireframes can also be used for feasibility checking purposes with LMS support specialists and learning designers to see if and what design ideas can be implemented given the existing technology toolkit.

Consider Navigation and Wayfinding
An online course interface involves user navigation starting at the course homepage and continuing into units that have nested lesson pages with links to other content, resources, and learning material. Course navigation is associated with information architecture and involves wayfinding. Wayfinding relates to how learners can navigate and move through the interface intuitively to find needed information and accomplish tasks. It starts at the top course homepage level and extends downward into lessons and throughout the entire course space. As wireframes become increasingly refined through successive iterations, they should gradually add wayfinding elements into their design. These include icons, arrow buttons, titling, labels on objects to help convey location, and other navigational controls in the interface designs.

Design Content Elements for Understandability
This strategy relates to information design, which spans a broad spectrum of message design features at all levels of the online course environment. When creating content to facilitate learner understanding, instructors or course designers need to become more sensitive to some of the following aspects

of information design and use them effectively to help learners focus their attention on important information and understand the content better:

- Color used to highlight and focus learner attention on important content elements
- Format and presentation of textual material on content pages using chunking and text blocking strategies
- Arrangement and grouping of screen elements such as using bullets and white space to visually separate different information elements
- Topography such as bolding of important words and providing descriptive labels for text blocks
- Strategic placement and integration of words and graphics on the screen so learners process information in an integrated way
- Orderly and familiar arrangements of content material within different sections of the interface, used consistently throughout the site

Instructors creating their own content will likely benefit from Horn's (1998a, 1998b) principles of structured writing mentioned earlier. Chunking and blocking strategies for instructional text material can be used consistently on lesson content pages to improve readability and comprehension. Information blocks may be used for presenting concepts, principles, processes, and procedures and can incorporate diagrams, tables, flow charts, and a variety of graphical elements to aid in the presentation of ideas.

Create Functional Prototypes to User Test

At some point in the interface design process the time comes to transition from paper wireframes and mockups to semiusable prototypes on the computer screen. These prototypes should have the major structural components of the various course pages in place. These prototypes should not be graphically polished and many of the course content elements may still be in development. The course homepage including top-level unit menus and lesson-level menus should be completed, along with at least one lesson in rough draft form depicting its structure and key informational elements and possibly including placeholder text and graphics. The purpose of a functional prototype is to show others, particularly students, and have them use it to perform simple, common tasks typical of a real course. One useful strategy is to ask users to "think aloud" as they look at and explore the course site, encouraging them to freely comment on what they see and how they feel, assessing the intuitiveness of the navigation and whether the interface provides all the information they need. Prototyping is an iterative process and adjustments and modifications can be made in the interface quickly between different user testers until a satisfactory learner experience is achieved.

Enhance the Graphical Look and Feel

One of the final phases in the interface design process involves what many interface design professionals call the "surface layer" of the user experience (Garrett, 2011). This is where aesthetics related to the visual treatment of text, graphics, and the fine-tuning of navigation elements come into play. Most LMSs offer limited capabilities in customizing the look and feel of online course interfaces. Course designers may be required to use standardized templates for their institution. However, there are still opportunities for enhancing the graphical layer of the interface. It is a good idea to have a person with some graphic design skill review the entire interface to give advice and, if possible, "polish up" some of the interface's graphical elements related to color usage, look and feel of navigational controls, and any multimedia material used to present content material.

The Holistic Mental Model of the Course Structure and Learner Interface

Following many of the design principles and strategies covered in this chapter will help set the stage for a more learner-centered design of the online course environment. The learner experience in an online course is often viewed as a journey that is significantly influenced by the design of this aspect of the online environment. To summarize what we have covered in this chapter, an ideal learner journey into the course structure and interface could be described as follows:

> Learners enter the online learning space and immediately notice the major structural elements of the environment starting with how the course content units are meaningfully structured and titled. It makes sense and flows logically. Learners begin exerting cognitive efforts and easily form a coherent mental model of how the learning environment is organized and how it works. They know where they are in the virtual space and can easily find their way around. Learners notice how information is clearly arranged on screens by scanning titles, headings, and pictures and noticing meaningful patterns. They can easily understand the content. Learners feel emotionally comfortable about the look and feel (aesthetics) and organization of the space, forming positive impressions about the space as one they feel good about revisiting frequently. Learners move about on the site at the behavioral level using navigational elements by clicking links and exploring functions that seem intuitively clear. They can quickly and easily get from one point in the environment to another. Learners seek out opportunities for social interactions in the virtual environment, especially the presence of instructors and peers. Overall, the course structure and learner interface design has met the needs of learners on all four dimensions of learning. The stage has been set for engaging and deep learning experiences to take shape.

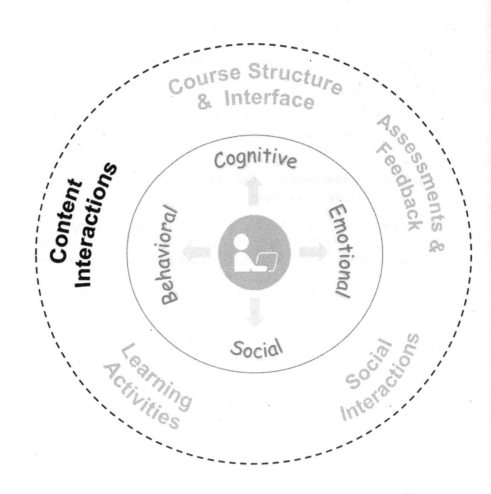

4

FACILITATING LEARNING THROUGH INSTRUCTIONAL CONTENT DESIGN

E very significant learning experience in an online course relates in some way to a learner's interaction with discipline-specific content. This chapter focuses on the design of learner–content interactions and applies concepts and principles from the integrated framework for designing the online learning experience. We approach this design aspect by first defining what we mean by instructional content interactions and common starting points for designing online course content. We also bring to light some common challenges and design factors influencing instructional content design in a digital learning environment. And finally, we present some fundamental shifts in designing online content material followed by practical strategies that can enhance learner–content interactions and foster higher levels of engagement and deeper learning outcomes.

Guiding Design Questions

- How can we start designing online content for different course design situations?
- How can we shift our thinking and practice to create pedagogically engaging content using new digital tools?
- How can we incorporate learning experience design strategies to create impactful learner–content interactions?

Beginning the Content Design Process

Online courses are content-rich environments, but instructional content is just one type of information within the online environment. In this section, we describe the type of content we focus on in this chapter and how instructors and course designers can acquire and develop it for their online courses.

Discipline-Specific Content Interactions

Online instructors provide course content that serves multiple pedagogical purposes that include communicating information about the course, providing guidance and instructions to students, facilitating discussion, teaching new knowledge and skills, and assessing student performance. Our focus, however, centers on discipline-specific instructional content that supports learning objectives. It concerns the design and presentation of the subject matter students in a course are expected to read, watch, listen to, and interact with.

Content for online courses can come from various sources and typically includes a mix of instructor-created, externally published, and curated materials. These materials can come in the form of published books and articles, instructor-produced documents, tutorials, case studies, interactive multimedia, videos, podcasts, live presentations (webinars), and other types of courseware materials. Most instructional content serves an explanatory function, helping learners acquire and enhance discipline-specific knowledge and skills. OERs and open web content produced by educators and subject matter experts constitute a growing source of course content. These open materials typically require repurposing and skillful integration into the curriculum.

The quality of online instructional material is largely determined by its design characteristics and how learners are required to interact with it. The level and type of learner interaction with instructional content ranges on a spectrum from passive rote learning, such as completing assigned readings and watching video lectures, to more active and effortful deep learning as when content material is paired with accomplishing challenging tasks and applying knowledge. In the online environment, learning experiences associated with learner–content interactions are heavily shaped by instructional design decisions around how to best use the affordances and capabilities of various online technologies and integrate these with instructional strategies for presenting content. For example, embedding knowledge check questions with corrective feedback into content presentations enables learners to better calibrate their learning and prevent inflated self-perceptions of what they know. Adding hypermedia links into and around digital documents enables learners to expand their understanding of concepts through related material and alternative modalities.

Starting Points for Online Content Design

The context within which instructors and course designers build online content varies widely depending on their situation. Different contexts involve different design challenges and strategies. Consider the following four course development scenarios and the content design requirements and challenges for each.

Enhance Content Design for an Existing Online Course

In this scenario, an instructor either inherits an online course or teaches an online course that requires content enhancements. Content redesign efforts to enhance the learner experience might include (a) expanding or condensing content, (b) reorganizing and reformatting content, (c) rewriting content for better understanding, (d) using new media to add interactivity, or (e) providing better integration between content units. This scenario usually requires a moderate amount of design and development effort depending on the qualitative improvements desired by instructors and course designers.

Convert and Repurpose Content From a Classroom-Based Course or Some Other Format to an Online Environment

In this scenario, redesign efforts often include rethinking the instructor's role and instructional strategies used to present and package content in an online environment. Content design activities might include repackaging and rewriting print materials and rethinking how to convert instructor classroom presentation materials and other classroom media assets into digital formats. Because the instructor in this scenario does not start from scratch, there is an opportunity to explore different types of learner–content interactions using new media formats and digital pedagogies. However, there are several content design challenges to be aware of in this situation.

Fostering learner engagement and creating flow, coherence, and contiguity of content in an online setting is often more difficult than anticipated. The most common tendency is to try to present content in a similar way to how it was done in a face-to-face course. From a learning experience design perspective, content extracted from a face-to-face course and transposed to the online context often lacks integration of the four dimensions of learning and its design may need to be rethought. Another challenge involves how to convey a sense of instructor presence either around or into the content material.

Curate and Integrate External Content Into a New or Existing Online Course

Content curation involves searching, vetting, and incorporating external learning resources created by other subject matter experts and integrating them into one's own online course. Resources might include ebooks, podcasts, simulations, games, blogs, entire courses, parts of courses with open use licenses, and other free or commercially purchased learning materials. Content sources may include content repositories or web resources such as YouTube, TED Talks, and OERs. Entire online courses have been built by assembling OERs and open web content. In most situations, it is helpful to enlist the support of campus librarians to assist in content searching, evaluating content quality, and working out copyright agreements with owners of published material and certain OERs.

For external content, the biggest design challenge usually involves integrating it into the online course structure and connecting it with other content units as seamlessly as possible. Externally produced content is often formatted differently, and integration into an LMS interface may be difficult. In addition, external content may not cover all desired material needed for important learning objectives or might contain excessive or unneeded information. Overall, this scenario usually involves a relatively small amount of content design and development work for instructors and course designers depending on the volume and type of materials selected.

Creating Online Content From Scratch
Developing new online content from the ground up with no previous course to build from requires comprehensive content research, design, and development. However, this scenario can provide opportunities to design new types of learner–content interactions and learning experiences, taking advantage of new digital technologies and pedagogies. It can often result in the most innovative learning designs for learner–content interactions. It can also involve a significant amount of design and development effort and probably should not be undertaken without instructional design, production, and technical support.

For all the scenarios described, the design thinking process can guide the content design and development process. This might include practices such as collaborating with learners, colleagues, and course designers throughout the design process using ideation, rapid prototyping, and testing out new content design approaches.

Factors Influencing Online Content Design Decisions

Every time a learner interacts with course content there is an opportunity to shape the learner experience for better or worse. The design thinking process begins by focusing on the learner experience and considering how other elements of the online learning environment influence that experience. We have

Figure 4.1. Factors influencing online content design decisions.

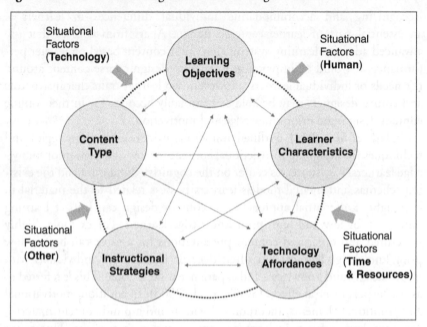

identified several factors of which to be cognizant when making design decisions about learner–content interactions. If we were to get inside the heads of skilled learning design thinkers and observe how they approach making content design decisions, we would likely notice them focusing on five key factors (illustrated in Figure 4.1 and discussed in the following subsections).

Learning Objectives

Developing course learning objectives is the starting point for all content design work. Learning objectives serve as pointers to the behaviors and cognitive skills learners will need to demonstrate. Objectives also indicate the type and scope of content learners need to acquire and how they will interact with it on the cognitive, behavioral, and social dimensions of learning. Having clear objectives for each unit, lesson, assignment, and learning activity guides content design efforts.

Without clear objectives, course content can become unfocused, excessive, and lead to unproductive learning experiences. The design of impactful learning experiences encourages emphasizing higher-order learning outcomes that connect knowledge with doing, essential for deep learning. In the integrated framework for designing the online learning experience presented in this book, it is assumed this crucial front-end step has already been completed.

Learner Characteristics

Recognizing and accommodating individual differences in learners is an essential part of learner-centered design. Apart from courses that use advanced adaptive learning systems that tailor content based on learner performance, it would be impractical to custom design course content around the needs of individual learners. However, two learner traits that instructors and course designers may be able to reasonably account for in their online content designs are prior knowledge and motivation.

Clark et al. (2011) outlined numerous evidence-based strategies and techniques for designing instructional content for low and high prior knowledge learners. Key strategies center on the cognitive dimension and the existing schemas and mental models learners possess related to the material to be taught. Differential approaches to content design can impact learning outcomes for low and high prior knowledge learners. For example, highly structured and organized content presentations for a topic can benefit low prior knowledge learners but often degrade learning for individuals with more background knowledge and experience on that topic. This is referred to as the "expert reversal effect" (Sweller et al., 2003). In addition, motivational and emotional elements, incorporated within and around content material, can stimulate and sustain learner attention and mental effort. This factor relates mostly to the cognitive and emotional dimensions of learning in the integrated framework for designing the online learning experience.

Content Type

Course content consists of a variety of different types of information. There are five dominant information types that comprise most educational content which includes facts, concepts, procedures, principle structures, and processes (Horn, 1989; Williams, 1977). These distinct information types require differential approaches and design strategies to communicate effectively. For example, content that involves structural information consisting of component parts of a system or spatial relations, as in a microscopic or physical structure, is best represented through visual illustrations. Similarly, content involving processes are best conveyed through diagrammatic representations and flow charts. Conceptual information requires definitions that highlight critical attributes with examples and nonexamples (Horn et al., 1969). Identifying the type of information to be conveyed within course units and topics (considered in tandem with learning objectives) enables instructors and course designers to match content type with the most efficient and optimal way to represent it for learners. The type of information also influences media selection. This factor is concerned mostly with the cognitive dimension of learning within the integrated framework for designing the online learning experience.

Instructional Strategies

Instructional strategies involve pedagogical approaches used to present content and facilitate a learning process. The quality of learner–content interactions in the online environment is heavily influenced by an instructor's choice of instructional strategies. In fact, the purported benefits of using certain digitally enabled multimedia to deliver instructional content often has more to do with the instructional strategies used than with the technology (Clark & Feldon, 2014). The following instructional strategies serve as broad influences in the design and presentation of online content:

- *Inductive strategies* include problem-based, inquiry-oriented, guided discovery, and project-based learning. Instructors and course designers can create content interactions that prompt learner curiosity, spark discovery, and encourage deeper thinking. In using this strategy, content supports learners as they address challenging questions, analyze case studies, or engage in social discourse around a topic. This strategy can integrate the four dimensions of learning around learner–content interaction.
- *Didactic strategies* involve direct instruction and packaging of online content presented in the form of structured explanatory presentations such as live webinars, videos, or recorded PowerPoint lectures and readings. This strategy emphasizes the cognitive dimension of learning and is most effective when learners have an intrinsic or immediate need for the information presented.
- *Active learning strategies* involve learners in "doing-type" activities (Horton, 2012) in which content interactions are paired with completing certain learning activities. These strategies call for different approaches to designing learner–content interactions and attempt to alleviate the passive and rote learning tendencies of most conventional learner–content interactions. This strategy can integrate the four dimensions of learning around learner–content interactions. It is used more extensively in designing learning activities, covered in the next chapter.

In the online environment, hybrid forms of content interactions that combine new digital media formats with a blending of instructional strategies enable the creation of more impactful learning experiences that many instructors and course designers have yet to recognize.

Technology Affordances

Designing learner–content interactions can take advantage of the capabilities of new digital media and technologies in presenting and packaging online course content. Newer software tools enable instructors and course designers to author their own courseware materials, creating modules and lessons that use a range of digital media formats. Video, hypertext and hypermedia, podcasts, graphics, data visualization, interactive multimedia (games and simulations), and virtual reality can be used alone or in combination in crafting engaging learner–content interactions.

There are many new technology-enabled options for creating online content interactions that can revitalize outdated strategies such as the infamous recorded PowerPoint lecture. One key strategy, discussed later, involves understanding the kinds of learner–content interactions inherent in the capabilities of new technology tools and using these in a hybrid way to enhance the learning experience. One caution though about new instructional technologies: it is easy to become enamored with features of technology tools and slip into a technology-centered mindset, losing sight of a learner-centered focus.

Situational Factors

Considering all the factors influencing online content, there are other situational factors that come into play in making content design decisions. These situational factors include, but are not limited to, three main categories: technology, human, and time and resource.

Technology

This factor refers to the technical aspects of an institution's learning ecosystem, which includes an LMS and available content design tools. Both provide capabilities and constraints on how content material can be presented, packaged, and accessed by learners. For example, an LMS can provide efficient ways to create, display, and access content, but can impose rigid constraints on how instructors and course designers can create content and how learners can interact with it. The same goes for rapid content development tools, whether commercial or home grown, that need to integrate with the LMS.

Human

This factor refers to people and the processes they adopt in online course development and design. When crafting learner–content interactions using new digital tools, the contributions of technical and design support staff can be invaluable in designing learning experiences. However, we need to underscore that applying learning experience design principles requires a significant shift in thinking and practice. Some support staff may be locked into established content design processes and practices that are not learner-centered or learning experience design-focused. It is common to encounter resistance from colleagues and campus leaders who support learner-centered and learning experience design in theory but not so much in practice.

Time and Resources

At first, efforts in designing and developing more learner-centered content material may require additional time and resources. There is an ROI factor that needs to be seriously considered. The payoffs of adopting learning experience design practices will be greater learning gains, increased learner engagement, and improved learner satisfaction with their coursework. These are often difficult to measure. Design efforts should focus first on specific learning goals and types of course content that could result in the greatest learning gains and quality enhancements of the learning experience. The general rule is to invest in the design of content interactions around complex content material that students most often struggle with involving higher-order learning objectives.

There is no one best way to design learner–content interactions for the online environment. Considering the different starting points for course content design and the five factors, each course design situation is unique and the need for design thinking is fundamental for developing the best possible solutions. Those desiring to put into practice the integrated framework for designing the online learning experience need to make several shifts in the way they think about and approach the design of learner–content interactions. This we cover in the next section before delving into specific design strategies.

Five Shifts for Designing Impactful Learner–Content Interactions

Well-designed online course content incorporates learning experience design principles that lay the groundwork for increased learner engagement and deeper learning. We now identify and briefly describe five key shifts that instructors and course designers need to make in their thinking and practice to craft more pedagogically effective learner-centered content for online courses. In the next section, we present several design strategies that build on these shifts.

A Shift From Fragmentation to Integration of Learner–Content Interactions

Fragmentation of the learning process can occur at all levels of online course design. The fragmentation of the learning experience can be first noticed at the course structure and interface aspect, then extending to the design of instructional content. Course units and lessons often consist of lists of assignments, readings, resources, and other content materials arranged around topic categories. The interconnections and coherence between disparate content elements within lessons will make perfect sense to instructors and experts in the discipline; but to novice learners, who have yet to acquire mental models related to the domain, these relationships may not be so obvious. Constructing knowledge from multiple content sources requires cognitive integration or cross-learning between different course materials and related topics (Rouet & Britt, 2014). Many learners, however, are unable to automatically make these connections and are often unaware of their own weak conceptual associations. Medina (2014) referred to this as the "binding challenge," where discrete content elements appear fragmented to novice learners and not bound together into cohesive neural networks or cognitive structures. Addressing this type of content-cognitive fragmentation requires extra effort on the part of instructors and course designers to make the connections explicit for learners.

One shift needed to design more integrated learner–content interactions is to provide greater explicitness as to how disparate content materials interrelate. This also includes providing greater transparency about an instructor's intention behind having learners engage with specific content (Felten & Finley, 2019). With complex content, many learners benefit from external supports to facilitate integration of knowledge acquired from separate content sources into more holistic mental models (Rout & Britt, 2014). Design strategies that support content integration can come in the form of embedding brief consolidation material and activities in and around content elements to promote integration (Britt & Sommer, 2004). The need for these types of integrators becomes more acute as online instructors and course designers incorporate OERs, which come from multiple sources into their courses. One strategy that addresses this content fragmentation issue is the use of pedagogical wrappers as content integrators. They are presented to learners prior to a content interaction or learning activity. They not only provide learners with information about how topics and content material interrelate but also make an instructor's pedagogical intent for a specific content interaction more explicit and meaningful to learners.

A Shift From Broad-Brush to Finely Targeted Content

In online courses, where it becomes easy for instructors and course designers to provide links to a vast digital repository of information, learners often become overwhelmed with content. In addition, instructors and course designers often invest considerable time and effort developing supplemental custom content. Examples might include PowerPoint lecture recordings, videos, podcasts, tutorials, and live virtual presentations. The bulk of this content consists mainly of explanatory information. In an information-rich digital learning ecosystem, online instructors and course designers need to become more strategic in selecting and developing course content.

This strategy shift involves focusing explanatory content acquisition and development on specific types of information that provide the greatest ROI in terms of learning gains and meeting student learning needs. It is important to acknowledge that learner interactions with the most explanatory instructional material, regardless of media format, generally produce minimal learner engagement and minimal learning gains (Wittwer & Renkl, 2008). However, Wittwer and Renkl (2008) discovered an exception to this phenomenon. Explanatory presentations can have a greater instructional impact if they specifically focus on teaching concepts and principles that support higher-order thinking and are tightly coupled with challenging learning tasks. In contrast, learning gains are lowest when explanatory material focuses on facts and information that are not task-related. Explanations of concepts and principles, two of the information types mentioned previously, are especially valuable for learners during the initial stages of acquiring new knowledge and skills.

This shift represents a quality over quantity strategy in providing instructional content. Offering a smaller number of finely tuned content materials, focused on teaching essential concepts and principles and how to apply them to various course-related activities and tasks, should underlie the process of curating and producing custom instructional content. Instructor-created PowerPoint lectures, information-based tutorials, and reading material containing extraneous "nice to know" information should be rethought and replaced with more modular content units that explain complex concepts and principles. Becoming more targeted at specific types of information in providing custom instructional content can mitigate some of the information overloading which has become characteristic of many online courses.

A Shift From Decontextualized to Contextualized Content

Instructors and course designers frequently emphasize covering as much subject material as possible and look for the most efficient ways to do this. Consequently, instructional methods often lean toward presenting subject matter as decontextualized abstract knowledge, skills, concepts, and definitions removed from situations and contexts in which the knowledge is applied (Grabinger & Dunlap, 1995). This is not a matter of knowledge being taken out of context as much as it is that most course content presented to learners has no context. The downside is that if the knowledge learners acquire is not explicitly connected to relevant problem-solving, tasks, and application activities, it remains inert and disembodied.

This shift in designing learner–content interactions involves making greater efforts to link course content material with relevant real-world situations. The instructional strategy supporting this shift is referred to as *contextualization* (Giamellaro, 2017). Infusing context into the presentation of content can be achieved when instructors and course designers deliberately incorporate stories, case studies, scenarios, simulation games, challenging tasks, and problem-based learning activities into their courses. It can also be accomplished through content material that includes multiple examples of how key concepts and principles are applied in real-world situations. Instructional content designed around walkthroughs of how an expert thinks about and approaches a variety of discipline-related problems is another contextualization strategy. Explanations of technical concepts can be more meaningful when instructional content is presented in ways that refer to simulated or real-world events. In courses that are more skill- and competency-based, content is almost always linked to supporting tasks and job performance. Such strategies foster greater cognitive, behavioral, and emotional engagement and can also interconnect with the social dimension of learning through group sharing of learning experiences.

A Shift From Single Media to Hybridized Media Content

Learner–content interactions in the online environment are technology-mediated and use a variety of digital media formats and instructional methods to convey course information. New digital tools for producing media content enable the creation of richer, more interactive kinds of content material than ever before. Given the plethora of available digital tools, online course content often falls short of taking advantage of the capabilities and affordances of tools that go overlooked by most online instructors and course designers.

One of the barriers to innovation in online content design is the result of functional fixedness caused by outmoded notions of instructional media. In this digital age, the distinctions between different media types have become blurred and conflated. Old media classification schemes rooted in an audio-visual-text paradigm no longer serve well in an internet-based digital learning ecosystem. For example, the internet, as the new dominant medium, can use and integrate all other media types as its content. In turn these new digital media types can use multiple other media types as their content. For example, internet video is now interactive and 3D, an amalgam of narrated PowerPoint slides, animations, television broadcasts, webinars, vodcasts, educational films, and recorded and live classroom lectures. Likewise, digital documents, web pages, blogs, and wikis can include embedded multimedia elements into their pages, including videos, animated charts and graphics, voice recordings, and quiz questions. Case studies and scenarios, typically associated with text-based documents, when converted to digital formats, can include embedded videos, graphics, question-answer objects, hyperlinks to related information, and branching. These new hybrid instructional content genres can provide learning experiences that seamlessly integrate all four dimensions of learning, providing learners with more engaging and impactful content interactions. Tools to create these digital content materials require minimal technical expertise and are available to most online instructors and course designers, either free or reasonably priced, with content seldom used to its full potential. For those interested in creating richer and more impactful learning experiences, this emerging media hybridization marks a time for new aspirations and standards for digital content design.

A Shift From Cognitive Dominance to Emotional and Behavioral Interplay

Despite best efforts to present content material in an organized and clear way, learners who are not motivated tend to perform poorly on knowledge acquisition tests (Bolkan et al., 2016). Cognitive engagement, necessary for deep learning, is interwoven with and fueled by emotional factors related to motivation (Feldon et al., 2019). Although this fact has been known by educators for decades, it is rare to see it applied seriously to learning design in higher education, especially in online courses. Keller and Burkman (1993) insisted that instructors and course designers need to consider the emotional appeal of every part of an instructional message, beginning when a learner first encounters the content and extending throughout the entire interaction. Educational game designers apply this principle such that the learner-player experience goes hand-in-hand with all content interactions.

This shift toward achieving greater cognitive and emotional connections in content design brings into play connections with the behavioral dimension of learning. The behavioral dimension is rooted in both cognitive processes and emotional undercurrents. In their research on the "Knowing–Doing Gap" in business organizations, Pfeffer and Sutton (2000) faulted higher education courses that consist mainly of content assimilation followed by graded discussion forums. They argued that these instructional approaches, also common in online courses, emphasize "sounding smart" over doing and action. As reported in chapter 1 of this book, the gap between what course graduates know and what they can do with their acquired course knowledge extends into the professional work world with negative repercussions.

The most impactful learning experiences occur when instructional content is designed in ways that arouse and sustain interest, promote invested mental effort, and connect knowing with doing. Adding to this, opportunities for learners to engage in social discourse during and after their content interactions provides for a balanced interplay of the four dimensions of learning, resulting in more holistic and fulfilling learning experiences. Next, we look at several strategies and examples in which these shifts in approaching the design of learner–content interactions can be implemented.

Strategies for Designing Learner–Content Interactions

In this section, we present several strategies and examples for crafting instructional content that builds on the design shifts from the previous section. We will look at strategies for content integration; media and method hybridization; contextualization; and combining the cognitive, emotional, and behavioral dimensions into content design. These strategies are not to be approached as prescriptions but rather starting points requiring design thinking to adapt and apply to a variety of learning design situations.

Use Pedagogical Wrappers to Integrate Content

Many online courses display lists of assigned content materials (readings, videos, tutorials, and online resources) that from a learner's perspective can appear as an arbitrary list of tasks to check off. In the previous section, we showed how learners often struggle to see critical interrelationships and connections between disparate content material and topics that to them may seem loosely connected. Instructors and course designers, however, can provide metacognitive support through incorporating pedagogical wrappers into and around assigned content interactions. These serve a priming and integration function to help learners engage more deeply with course material and better integrate the knowledge they acquire. Pedagogical wrappers also help students understand, from an instructor perspective, the pedagogical rationale, relevance, and learning goals for content-related assignments and activities (Felten & Finley, 2019).

Pedagogical wrappers in online courses can come in different forms. They often take the shape of concise text-based descriptors presented before a learner engages in an assigned content interaction or learning activity. They

Figure 4.2. Ways for designing meaningful learner-centered pedagogical wrappers.

The What-Why-How Wrapper Formula

The content of a pedagogical wrapper concisely answers three questions. (A two- to three-sentence descriptor for each question is often sufficient.)

1. **What** is the subject or topic of the assigned content material?
2. **Why** has it been assigned, and what is its relevance and connection with other course materials and learning objectives?
3. **How** should content be approached, and what's most important to focus on? (If learners need to focus mainly on a few sections or portions of a reading or video, let them know it.)

For complex content material or learning activities, pedagogical wrappers can be more elaborate, containing statements of learning objectives. Also consider including a list of questions students should be able to answer following the assignment to encourage purposeful reading, viewing, or listening.

Message Style and Tone

Conciseness is important. Time invested in writing pedagogical wrappers should be proportional to the complexity and importance of the learning material or activity. If an item is too long and formalized, learners will likely not read it. Make it interesting by using a personal and conversational writing tone and style that conveys instructor presence.

---

can be spatially positioned on the course website proximal to links that open assigned course material, and in some cases placed within the content itself. For more complex content material and a more personalized approach, a brief instructor video or audio recording can introduce the content. Pedagogical wrappers have several core attributes, which are outlined in Figure 4.2.

Creating concise pedagogical wrappers requires minimal time and resources. They not only help learners better connect and integrate related instructional content but also encourage instructors and course designers to be more explicit and learner-centered in how they design learner–content interactions. We encourage online instructors and course designers to experiment with creating pedagogical wrappers using various media formats and personal approaches.

Integrate Rich Content Interactions Through Hybrid Multimedia and Instructional Methods

Earlier we underscored the pedagogical limitations and shortcomings of explanatory instructional content. However, most studies revealing poor learning outcomes from explanatory instructional material have focused mainly on conventional single media approaches and didactic instructional methods. The design shift discussed previously involves media hybridization where new digital pedagogies enable the creation of instructional content that interweaves multiple media formats and instructional methods. The key to the hybridization strategy involves capitalizing on the strengths of different media for conveying specific content types and content interactions in combination with instructional methods that support learning objectives.

Figure 4.3 shows the screen from a hybridized online content module in which several design attributes can be noted. Throughout the content module instructor presence is conveyed through personalized text with photos, video, and audio recordings. The modality of instructor communication can change throughout a module depending on the type of content to be communicated and the learning task.

Media elements used on any page (text, graphics, videos, and audio) are selected and crafted based on the type of information and cognitive

Figure 4.3. Science microlearning module.

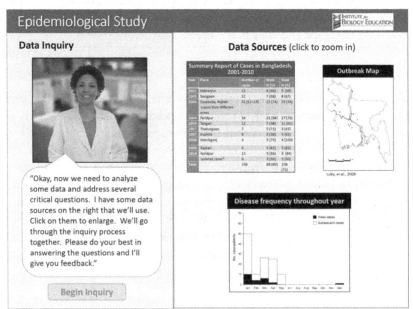

engagement necessary to maximize learning of specific content (Clark et al., 2011). Video material is not used continuously on every page but is reserved for content involving dynamic processes. Instructional text is used frequently on slides where the content interaction calls for slower and deeper processing. When instructor text is used in place of video or audio, the tone and style is informal and conversational. Although these content modules are often linear, frequent changes in how content is presented along with different types of learner–content interactions sustain learner attention and reduce boredom and habituation (Keller & Burkman, 1993; Simon, 2016). This approach contrasts with other common online presentations that consist of a steady stream of similarly formatted slides coupled with continuous audio or video commentary. Interactions with different information types are interwoven into content that includes charts, graphs, diagrams, animations, videos, and periodic knowledge check questions with feedback. Reflection prompts, links to more detailed content, and embedded elements from the web can also be interwoven, creating a rich learner–content interactive experience.

The digital hybrid design strategy overcomes many of the pedagogical deficiencies mentioned earlier with explanatory presentations. These modules can be packaged in the form of hypermedia documents or slide-based formats. The key to creating pedagogically robust online explanatory presentations requires a holistic design mindset that integrates lesson content types and objectives, instructional strategies, and technology affordances.

Increase Cognitive Engagement and Motivation Through Emotional Design

Research-based principles for designing online learning content focus mainly on message design strategies for managing learner cognitive load (Clark et al., 2011; Mayer, 2014). This bias toward the cognitive dimension of learning overlooks the essential emotional dimension in learning design. Efforts to improve the clarity and organization of instructional content to support better cognitive processing are only half the story (Calvo & D'Mello, 2011). Arousing and sustaining learner attention and provoking effortful mental processing are rooted in the emotional dimension of learning and expressed through motivation. Traditionally, motivation has been viewed primarily as the learner's responsibility. However, in learning experience design, it is also the instructor's responsibility to activate the emotional dimension to improve cognitive engagement.

One of the most comprehensive research-supported strategies for building motivational elements into the learning design process is the attention, relevance, confidence, and satisfaction (ARCS) model developed by Keller

(1999). Applying ARCS as a strategy for incorporating emotional and motivational elements into the design and presentation of online content can include some of the following strategies.

Attention
Before learners engage with content material, stimulate interest and curiosity and challenge or introduce incongruity, mystery, or conflict around the content. Some of this can be done in the pedagogical wrappers around the content material.

Relevance
Before presenting the instructional content, emphasize how the material has meaning and is related to learning goals and student interests. Motivation increases when course assignments are worded and framed around student personal goals (Vansteenkiste et al., 2006).

Confidence
As learners interact with challenging and complex content, instructors and course designers need to be sensitive to certain learner characteristics such as self-efficacy. Learners who have self-doubts about their abilities to understand certain content material need encouragement to persist throughout a learning task. Simply informing students upfront, before interacting with difficult content, to expect some struggles often helps mitigate the debilitating effects of low self-efficacy (Felten & Finley, 2019).

Satisfaction
In addition to extrinsic reinforcement for completing content-related assignments, providing students with opportunities to apply what they have learned promotes feelings of satisfaction. This underscores the interconnection among the cognitive, emotional, and behavioral dimensions of learning emphasized throughout this book.

Expanding on Keller's (1999) strategies for capturing and sustaining learner attention, recent research in cognitive studies and neuroscience has shown that inducing states of curiosity in learners can have positive influences for learning. When content material is presented in ways that include elements of surprise, novelty, gaps in knowledge, and moderate levels of complexity, learning and memory retention are improved (Oudeyer et al., 2016). Curiosity activates systems in the brain related to learning and induces motivation to acquire knowledge about a topic (Kidd & Hayden, 2015). Building curiosity and mystery around course content can be introduced in pedagogical wrappers and sustained by instructors through periodic nudges in discussion forums to stimulate learner–content engagement at a deeper level.

One emotional and motivational letdown for many learners as they encounter instructional content is how learning objectives are presented at the outset of a learning interaction. Most objective statements are written using terms learners have yet to fully understand until they complete the assignment. Objectives are written primarily for the instructor and course designers as tools to aid in course design. Not that learning objectives should be discarded; the problem is that most objectives pertaining to instructional content are not written in a learner-centered way. The objectives used by course designers can be translated and written in ways that provoke interest, curiosity, and a perception of relevance to learners about what the content material will do for them. Why not introduce a content-related assignment with some challenging questions, a puzzling compelling problem, or describe a mystery that the content will help clarify?

Building emotional and motivational elements into and around instructional content interactions often requires some creativity and design thinking. Making a deliberate effort to go beyond a cold cognitive approach and motivating learners throughout their content interactions is a fundamental strategy for designing engaging and impactful learning experiences.

Add Context to Content Through Stories and Scenarios

There are numerous strategies for designing engaging and impactful online learning experiences around instructional content. For example, Allen (2011) emphasized the four core elements of context, challenge, action, and feedback. A core principle underlying this strategy is the contextualization of instructional content that draws on real-world situations. An integral part of a contextualization strategy is the use of story to provide a compelling narrative within or around instructional content. Horton (2012), however, observed that despite their widespread use in classroom courses and the enrichment they contribute to learning experiences, online instructors and course designers seldom use stories.

Stories in and of themselves are often insufficient for conveying a complex subject matter and facilitating higher-level learning objectives. To be pedagogically effective, they need to be skillfully and tightly interwoven into the design of instructional content and learning activities. Given their potential to activate both the cognitive and emotional dimensions of learning and serve as a catalyst for social discourse, online instructors and course designers should make greater efforts to incorporate stories into instructional content interactions. We offer three strategies as starting points.

Integrate Stories Into and Around Instructional Content
Horton's (2012) eLearning design model identified several situations where stories can be most effectively used in content presentations. He recommended that stories be used to demonstrate applicability of the content, provide concrete instances and examples of the subject matter, and humanize content by showing its relationship and impact on people. Stories can be used in conjunction with online reading assignments. They can emotionally enrich material that has a pedantic and "cold cognitive" quality, adding relevance and interest to content.

Stories used in online courses can be developed by instructors based on their own professional experiences or obtained from recorded interviews with experts. The stories can be embedded within content material or linked from course topic and content units. However, a story disembedded from a related content unit in the form of a stand-alone digital recording or text requires integration and connection with related content material and tasks. To have a significant pedagogical impact on learning and performance, stories, like stand-alone pictures, need to be explicitly connected to course content and learning objectives. The most common narrative forms used in education include stories told by experts, case studies, scenarios, narrative-based simulation games, and vignettes.

Interweave a Story Throughout the Lesson's Content
Some instructors have used a story-centered approach in their course designs, in which a central narrative runs through an entire lesson's content (Paulus et al., 2006). The example in Figure 4.4 illustrates a unit of an online course centered around a fictitious case-based story anchored in an authentic real-world context. A short narrative is presented at the outset of the lesson, which unfolds as learners proceed through the unit. The narrative establishes a context involving characters and challenges that are further developed and integrated into lessons. Course content such as important concepts and principles are illustrated and given context through characters and the challenges presented in the story. At certain junctures in the lessons, the narrative becomes more complex and learners are presented with tough decisions which learners deliberate in discussion forums. The story narrative unfolds throughout the lesson and questions are posed by instructors on how the content (concepts and principles) can be applied in similar real-world situations. Integrated stories like this can provide a compelling and emotionally charged context for learner–content interactions involving both conceptual learning and knowledge application.

Figure 4.4. Real-world context introduced by short narrative.

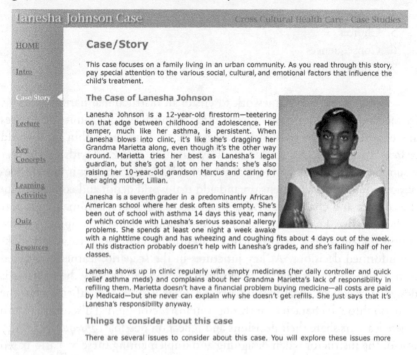

Add Context Through Crafting Compelling Scenario Narratives

The primary mental model in story design is the situation model (Busselle & Bilandzic, 2008). Focusing on challenging situations related to a discipline is a good place for instructors to begin in creating stories for their online courses. Stories based on a situational model can be referred to as scenarios or case scenarios. Crafting story narratives that go beyond simply arousing interest and motivation is typically not a skill set for many instructors and course designers.

One practical strategy for developing narrative content for scenarios, specifically aimed at higher-level learning goals and complex job-related tasks, involves the use of the 7Cs framework (Bundy & Howles, 2017). This framework can be used in a variety of online instructional contexts and can serve as the backbone for creating instructionally robust content interactions. Scenarios can be enhanced by incorporating interactive elements using the digital hybridization strategies presented earlier.

Seven Components of the Framework

1. Challenge
2. Context

3. Characters
4. Content
5. Choices
6. Consequences
7. Connections

Applying the 7Cs framework to create an instructional narrative begins by focusing on the learning objectives for a course lesson or unit. Objectives are reframed and converted into *challenges* that are situated within a real-world *context*. Interactive case scenarios always include *characters* with the learner assuming an active role as a central character. Various characters infuse the scenario with a personal dimension and add real-world depth and complexity to the context and challenge. Throughout the scenario decision-making is part of the narrative. Learners are asked to draw upon and apply discipline-specific course *content* and if needed acquire additional knowledge to aid in making informed decisions. At key junctures in the scenario, learners are asked to make *choices* reflecting their decisions. Depending on how the scenario is designed, feedback regarding learner decisions is provided either within the scenario through characters or through an instructor-guided discussion forum where learners share their decisions and reflect on possible *consequences*. A key role of the instructor when designing and implementing these scenario-based learning activities is to facilitate and build *connections* to foster deeper learning and promote knowledge transfer between the scenario experience, course content, and linkages to real-world situations portrayed in the scenario. Figure 4.5 shows a screen from an interactive case scenario where learners acquire knowledge for making decisions as they engage in an authentic situation.

The 7Cs framework is intended as a design aid for instructors and course designers who want to contextualize course content by crafting their own compelling story narratives. Simple case scenarios can be created with a variety of available software tools including PowerPoint. Skillfully designed case stories integrate all four learning dimensions, providing engaging and memorable learning experiences without the expense and complexity of developing games and simulations.

Content Is Not Enough; It Is in the Interaction Design

Through content interactions learners construct knowledge and develop skills. The development or enhancement of online content can involve repurposing of existing content, curation of external resources, and creation of custom material. The design of online instructional content can be influenced by a

Figure 4.5. Sample episode of an interactive case scenario.

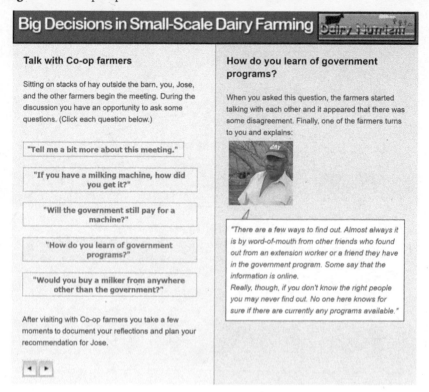

combination of factors including learning objectives, learner characteristics, content type, instructional strategies, technology affordances, and situational factors. The design shifts and strategies that underlie providing pedagogically robust learner–content interactions for online courses require design thinking that elevates the learner perspective above or at least on equal footing with "covering content." It involves strategies for better content integration, using pedagogical wrappers to connect content, integrating rich content interactions through hybrid multimedia and instructional methods, increasing cognitive engagement and motivation through emotional design, and adding context to content through stories and scenarios. Foundational to all of this is the ability to think holistically about the learner experience. Integrating the cognitive dimension with the often-neglected emotional dimension, linking content to behaviors and performing tasks, and incorporating social interactions around what has been learned are key ingredients for crafting engaging and deep learning experiences in the online environment.

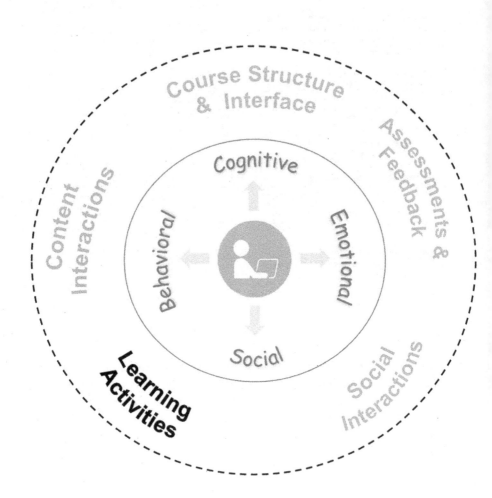

5

CREATING MEANINGFUL
LEARNING ACTIVITIES
THROUGH LEARNING
EXPERIENCE DESIGN

I n chapters 3 and 4, we focused on design strategies that optimize learner interactions with the technology interface and content aspects of the online learning experience. This chapter deals with one of the most pedagogically complex and vital aspects of online learning design: learning activities. Well-designed and challenging learning activities are the means through which learners construct new knowledge, build skills, exercise higher-order thinking, and connect what they have learned with their academic, professional, and personal lives.

We begin by describing key attributes and types of online *learning activities*. The emphasis throughout this chapter is on applying design thinking as a foundational strategy for creating innovative learning solutions that fully take advantage of technology affordances. Our goal is to provide exemplars, ideas, and strategies to stimulate one's own design creativity for crafting engaging and impactful learning activities in the online environment.

Guiding Design Questions

- How can we apply design thinking to create learning activities?
- How can we design engaging online learning activities?
- How can we integrate learning activities into a course unit to support higher-order learning?
- How can we design learning activities that help learners engage in deep learning?

Learning Activities, More Than Assignments

Although course instructors have a big picture understanding of how various content elements and assignments integrate into a course as a whole, learners might perceive individual assignments as disconnected tasks with only implicit relationships with other course material and practical application. Van Merriënboer and Kirschner (2018) described this as "atomistic" learning design characterized by fragmentation and compartmentalization of the learning process that can inhibit application and transfer of learning. An example of fragmentation is the common undergraduate course unit consisting of separate lectures, readings, discussions, quizzes, papers, projects, and practice exercises, which from a learner perspective may seem like loosely connected learning events. Online course designs that consist mainly of "assignment lists" are in many ways carryovers from face-to-face classroom-based instructional models. This type of course design does not provide the kinds of integrated and holistic learning experiences that engage learners and promote deep learning in an online environment.

Throughout this chapter, we use the term *learning activities* as opposed to *assignments*. The distinction between the two can be somewhat blurry but worth noting when designing online courses. Often, assignments are given to students as required stand-alone tasks to be completed as homework. In designing an online course, it is necessary to think more holistically about assignments and tasks as more active, inclusive, and engaging activities. Learning activities can be purposefully and skillfully designed as "learning experiences" that actively engage learners at the cognitive, emotional, behavioral, and social dimensions of learning. Therefore, we view *learning activities* as higher order and more complex learning experiences that typically incorporate all four learning dimensions, emphasizing both knowing and doing.

Types of Online Learning Activities

This chapter draws from existing frameworks for classifying and designing learning activities. Two widely used practitioner-focused frameworks that emphasize the learner experience aspects of course design have been provided by Horton (2012) and Fink (2013).

Horton (2012) identified three types of learning activities: absorb, do, and connect. Absorb-type activities are those in which the learner interacts with content and is mentally active in perceiving, processing, consolidating, considering, and judging. Absorb-type activities include content interactions that involve reading, listening, and viewing. Do-type activities are those that link content knowledge to application and skills. These activities involve practice exercises, discovery tasks, games, and simulations. Connect-type activities go beyond absorbing information and acquiring knowledge; they link newly acquired knowledge to real-world tasks through reflection, questioning, evaluation, research, and critique. This book expands on Horton's framework by integrating absorb, do, and connect activities in a more holistic way to avoid fragmentation.

Fink's (2013) framework provided a holistic approach to creating "significant" learning experiences that focus on active learning. Similar to Horton (2012), Fink identified the following main types of learning activities: (a) getting information and ideas through various media such as video lectures, texts, or web-based resources; (b) doing and observing through authentic learning activities such as case studies, simulations, and role plays; and (c) reflecting on what has been learned and the learning process, either alone or with others. Fink emphasized an integrated approach to learning experience design where his three types of learning activities are interwoven to form a "holistic view to create the kinds of learning activities capable of creating significant learning" (p. 118). Translating this holistic approach for designing learning activities into tangible learning experiences requires design thinking and integrated design strategies that bring together multiple learning tasks, including absorbing information, doing, connecting, and reflecting into a single unified learning experience. Incorporating the four dimensions of learning into the design of these types of learning activities can result in deeper, more engaging, and significant learning outcomes.

Designing integrated learning activities that combine absorbing discipline-related information, doing, reflecting, interacting with others, and connecting what is learned to real-world contexts are major ingredients for creating impactful online learning experiences. In addition, these learning experiences need to incorporate a variety of motivational and engagement elements, optimal levels of challenge, contextualization (linkage to real-world situations), flow, active learning, interactivity, learner agency, and choice, all of which promote deep learning. Designing such learning experiences requires a new way of thinking.

A New Mindset for Designing Learning Activities for the Online Environment

The potential pedagogical payoff of designing significant learning activities for online courses requires instructors and course designers to acquire a better understanding of the affordances of new technology and adopt a new mindset for designing innovative and engaging learning activities.

Applying knowledge of technology affordances to create innovative learning solutions often occurs by drawing inspiration from other professional fields. Consider the design thinking used by creators of educational digital games. Game design focuses heavily on the player experience, which is equally important as the content contained in the game. Well-designed games, like most well-designed learning activities, present a compelling challenge that motivates players to fully invest in the experience. In many popular internet multiplayer games, one can observe how the four dimensions of learning (cognitive, emotional, behavioral, and social) are interwoven into an interactive and compelling experience. The design mindset and engagement strategies used in game design can be useful for instructors and course designers when developing learning activities (Kapp et al., 2014).

Designing Online Learning Activities

There are numerous approaches for designing online courses and learning activities, many of which involve following a systematic design process. One common approach is the ADDIE (analysis, design, development, implementation, and evaluation) model (Branch, 2009; Kurt, 2017). Although useful in designing learning activities in certain traditional classroom-based situations, the ADDIE model has proven to be less effective in producing innovative solutions for technology enabled learning environments. Newer and more flexible design approaches are better adapted for digital learning ecosystems and take greater advantage of the affordances of digital media and technology. An example is Allen's (2012) successive approximation method (SAM), which integrates design thinking and is less linear and fragmented and more holistic and iterative. Next, we provide an example scenario to illustrate and walk through the process for creating online learning activities using a design thinking process. Design thinking has proven to be most effective with small teams and approached as a collaborative activity (Brown, 2009).

French and Italian Renaissance Literature Course Design

For several years, Professor Janus had taught a successful classroom-based course in French and Italian Renaissance literature and received approval and funding to develop an online version of the course. He collaborated with the college's instructional technology team to set up a course framework and to create a set of online learning activities that used available digital technology in more innovative and pedagically effective ways.

Professor Janus's initial goal was to create a series of online lessons to develop student skills in critically reading specific genres of literary works from the French and Italian Renaissance period. Each lesson would focus on two or three short literary works that learners would be called on to analyze and interpret using a strategy called "intertextuality." This form of critical reading involves identifying relationships and inferences within a text with the art, religion, science, cultural artifacts, and other literary works of the author's time period. Learners analyze these intertextual relationships and explain how they influenced the author's work.

Critical reading for intertextuality requires significant invested mental effort involving higher-order cognitive skills such as analysis, synthesis, and evaluation. The learning outcomes desired require learner engagement and deep learning encompassing all four dimensions of learning. The initial design plan for the online course proposed replicating the existing face-to-face course lesson structure, which consisted of three separate but associated learning activities:

1. *Lecture presentation (45 minutes)*: intended to prepare learners for the critical readings, covering background information, explanations of terminology, and intertextuality influences that learners need to utilize
2. *Reading assignments*: two or three literary works downloadable as PDF documents from the course website that learners read and then answer several interpretive questions to be returned to the instructor
3. *Class discussions*: instructor-led debriefing of the readings to share interpretations and clarify misunderstandings

Replicating the structure of these existing lessons and learning activities for online delivery would involve producing video lectures, creating electronic documents and question submission forms, and setting up an instructor-moderated online discussion forum. Because Professor Janus was not satisfied with the learning outcomes and level of learner engagement experienced in the classroom version of the course, he wanted to explore the use of available digital technologies to redesign these lessons and improve the quality of the learner experience. The design process for creating the new online learning activities involved six phases of design thinking. We describe next how he created these learning activities using the design thinking process.

Empathize With Learners

To develop a better understanding of how learners approach critical reading tasks, Professor Janus decided to use the existing lesson structure from the classroom version of the course as a starting point to probe deeper into the learner experience. Professor Janus, together with a student assistant, arranged meetings with five current and former students from the face-to-face course. Questions focused on each of the three component learning tasks comprising the critical reading lessons: lecture presentation, reading assignments, and class discussions. These meetings, lasting about 20 minutes each, were informal and conversational in tone, and structured around several prompt questions to start the conversation.

During office hours for his classroom course, Professor Janus looked for opportunities to briefly chat with additional students regarding what they thought and felt about the learning activities. In addition, during one class session, he divided students into small groups and asked them to list their major likes and dislikes with the critical reading assignments and offer suggestions on how to make the learning experience better. This took about 15 minutes of class time. The quality of the feedback was eye-opening, providing insights that would be useful not only in the design for the new online learning activities but also for enhancing the face-to-face course.

Define the Design Challenge

Together with a student assistant and an instructional technology consultant, Professor Janus analyzed and synthesized the learner feedback and constructed several personas—fictional characters that represent characteristics of students in the course. As a result of this process, the design team formed a more accurate mental picture of learner challenges and envisioned how they experienced the learning activities in terms of the four dimensions of learning. The common themes that emerged are summarized in Table 5.1.

The two major issues disclosed by students centered around cognitive load and fragmentation of lesson components. Lecture content material was perceived as most useful for learners at the time of greatest need which was during the actual critical reading task. Constant task switching between lecture notes and the reading material created a type of split attention effect (Clark & Mayer, 2016) that interrupted the flow of deep reading, resulting in frustration and poor comprehension.

The learning process was also perceived by students as fragmented or broken down into separate related events that were not tightly integrated into a unified experience. Overall, the learning activities within the lesson were not experienced as engaging and felt more like required assignments: read the article, answer test questions and submit answers to the instructor, and discuss the reading. The discussions did not address many of the interpretive challenges that occurred during the time of the reading.

The insights gained from learner feedback set the stage for the next phase of the design thinking process, which was to articulate the pedagogical

TABLE 5.1
Synthesis of Feedback Gained From Students

Learning Activities	*Students' Feedback*
Lecture Presentation	• The instructor conveyed enthusiasm and passion for the literary works in the lectures, which was motivating for learners. • Although lectures were perceived by many students as passive learning experiences and attention often waned, most of the lecture materials were perceived as useful for helping to interpret intertextual relationships in the literary pieces.
Readings Assignments	• Readings were cognitively challenging and complicated. Intertextual connections were difficult to identify and interpret even after being explained during the lecture. This was the hardest part of the entire course for most students. Attention and interest often declined during the reading activity and a few students confessed they read superficially only to answer the questions. • Referencing lecture notes and course website resources during the actual reading were disruptive and broke the flow of the reading experience (split attention effect). • Understanding terminology was one of the biggest frustrations, requiring learners to frequently break the reading flow to look up words and phrases. One student mentioned that it would be very helpful to be able to get hints and tips as one read the literary pieces. • Responding to the instructor's questions was difficult and stressful and felt like a test. Not being able to get feedback on their responses left them unable to gauge if their interpretations were accurate. This was the least enjoyable aspect of the learning activity.
Class Discussions	• Many students completed the critical readings still in an uncertain state regarding their interpretations. The follow-up discussions provided clarity and an opportunity for the instructor to probe more deeply into texts. • For many students, this deeper understanding seemed to come after the fact. To have the "a-ha!" occurring during the time of the reading would provide a much more satisfying experience.

challenges to be addressed in the design of the online version of the course. Rather than moving quickly to coming up with solutions to these design challenges, the team took time to frame the learning design challenges into the form of "How can we . . ." questions:

- How can we create a better flow experience for learners when they engage in critical reading of the text material?
- How can we make the necessary support information provided during the lecture more easily and quickly accessible to learners as they read the texts and minimize split attention?
- How can we make the interpretive tasks associated with the readings seem more engaging and challenging?
- How can we make the questions following a critical reading activity seem more compelling and less like test questions?
- How can we make the three main components of the lesson feel less fragmented and more tightly integrated?
- How can we make the discussion more relevant and engaging for individual learners?

Formulating these types of questions and resisting the temptation to jump immediately to solutions helped to focus the next phase in the design thinking process on coming up with creative ideas.

Ideate and Brainstorm a Variety of Potential Solutions

Professor Janus, along with a faculty associate, a student assistant, and an instructional technologist, convened for several short sessions to explore and brainstorm ideas to address the design challenge. The instructional technologist demonstrated a few hypermedia software products that sparked ideas about using the affordances of multimedia software to incorporate interactive text material. One design thinking strategy used to generate potential design solutions was to express each idea in the form of a "What if we could . . ." statement. This approach created synergy and ensured that numerous ideas were offered for consideration and avoided coming to closure on any one particular idea prematurely. The team's "What if . . ." statements included the following:

- What if we bring together or integrate the support information from the instructor lecture into the critical reading text so that the learners get the information they need far closer in time and space to where it's needed (absorbing, doing, and connecting into a single unified activity)?

- What if we incorporate hints and prompts into the text where they can aid the learner in interpretation?
- What if we make the interpretive questions associated with each reading seem more game-like by framing them as an interpretive challenge rather than a test?
- What if the interactive critical reading activity contained an assessment function?
- What if learners submit questions for the follow-up discussion during and immediately after the reading?

Brainstorming generated numerous creative ideas for using new digital software to design critical reading activities for the online course. The team selected several of the most promising ideas for refinement and prototyping. For example, it was suggested that portions of Renaissance literary texts could be displayed on webpages containing hyperlinks. As learners read the texts, they could click on these links that display popup windows containing embedded supportive background material, definitions of unfamiliar terms, multimedia explanatory content, and questions to provoke curiosity. This material might also include personalized instructor hints and tips in the form of text bubbles and audio and video clips. This would extend the instructor presence into and around the readings as a type of virtual critical reading coach. Other ideas included incorporating gamification elements into the learning activities to boost motivation and interest.

Several innovative approaches for designing pedagogically rich critical reading activities emerged from these brainstorming sessions. It became evident that the initial temptation to replicate the existing classroom course lessons online would have resulted in a less than optimal and fragmented learning experience that neglected to take advantage of the affordances of technology.

Prototype Design Ideas

The next phase of the design thinking process involved visualizing and refining some of the best ideas generated from the brainstorming sessions. This involved creating rapid prototypes, often referred to as storyboards or wireframes, to better visualize how an interactive critical reading activity might look and function. The rapid prototypes were "quick and dirty" mockups, often in the form of paper sketches depicting the major screen elements of the learner interface.

Over a period of several days, these prototype sketches were reviewed and refined by team members and shared with students and colleagues for feedback. Having something tangible but still in a rough form prompted

Figure 5.1. Screenshot of a prototype design.

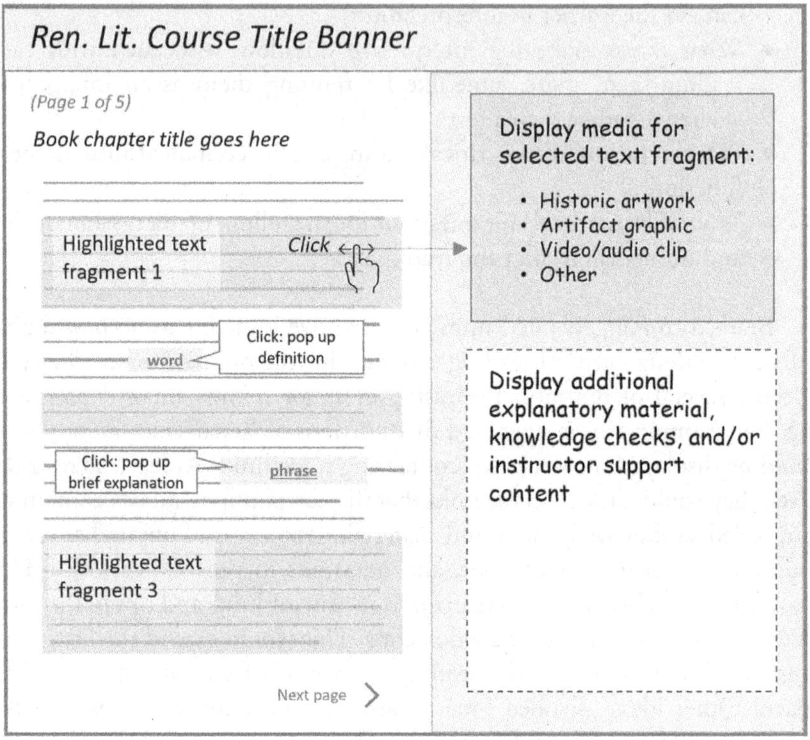

others to contribute ideas to a work in progress. Later, a simple but higher fidelity mockup of a critical reading interface to illustrate how it might look and function was created using PowerPoint slides. After several iterations and refinements, a final prototype design was completed that enabled the design team to walk through how a critical reading hypermedia document would look, function, and be used as a learning activity. An example PowerPoint prototype screen is provided in Figure 5.1.

Test Out Designs in the Real-World Context

The prototyping process enabled the learning technologist to identify an inexpensive and user-friendly software application that Professor Janus could use to create a variety of interactive documents for his online learning activities. The software had the ability to paste text from digitized documents of Renaissance literary works into the application, format it, and add interactive elements. For example, Professor Janus could highlight certain words, phrases, or portions of a text that when clicked displayed helpful interpretive support material, including definitions of unfamiliar words and expressions and historical artwork referred to in the text. Instructor explanatory commentary and knowledge-check questions with feedback could also be integrated at certain key points in the document for learners to self-assess their critical reading accuracy.

Implement

Professor Janus developed a process for creating multiple critical reading learning activities such that each weekly lesson in the course included at least one critical reading activity. Figures 5.2 and 5.3 show screens from the final course. The final solution addressed the design challenges, resulting in a set of learning activities that integrate disparate learning tasks into a holistic online learning experience. The structure of each learning activity consisted of the following interrelated components:

- *Introductory pedagogical wrapper:* This introduces the learning activity including a brief instructor video providing a broad historical context for the reading and an explanation of the purpose of the critical reading (see Figure 5.2). The tone of the introduction was presented in a highly enthusiastic and motivational fashion, framing the reading activity like an interpretive mission going back in time.
- *Interactive hypermedia document containing a portion of a literary work:* Each reading begins with one or two interpretive challenges to reinforce the critical reading task. The hypermedia material contains highlighted text with embedded interactive elements. These elements provide scaffolding for students to detect intertextuality relationships in the text and reinforce critical reading skills (see Figure 5.3).
- *Critical reading challenge questions:* When learners complete a reading they are prompted to respond to the interpretive challenges for the reading. This consists of a link to the quizzing application of an LMS which presents a few short answer and multiple choice questions to check student critical reading skills and to validate completion of the activity.
- *Follow-up group discussion:* The instructor sets up and moderates a discussion forum to debrief the interactive reading experience. The discussion provides learners with an opportunity to reflect on their challenges interpreting the literary work and share their insights with others.

The design thinking phases and action steps used in the French and Italian Renaissance literature online course generated a novel hybrid learning experience and is summarized in Table 5.2. Lecture content unbundled and integrated into the actual reading task enabled acquiring information at the time of greatest need to support critical reading skills.

Figure 5.2. Screenshot of introduction activity with video.

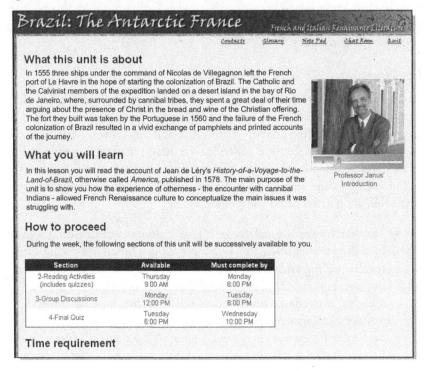

Strategies for Designing Online Learning Activities

We offer five strategies for designing online learning activities. These strategies are not intended to provide prescriptions but rather spark ideas for crafting learning through the use of design thinking and taking advantage of technology affordances.

Apply Design Thinking With an Empathic Mindset for the Learner

The foundation of design thinking is empathy (Brown, 2009). In practicing learning experience design, empathy is more than just understanding and acknowledging the feelings of struggling learners; it involves a learner-centered mindset coupled with behaviors that reflect what we refer to as the four Cs of empathic design:

1. *Caring:* This is a genuine concern about the pedagogical impact of a particular learning activity, how learners experience it and, if needed, a desire to make it better. But caring needs to involve a deeper desire to understand more about the learner perspective.

Figure 5.3. Screenshot of interactive text.

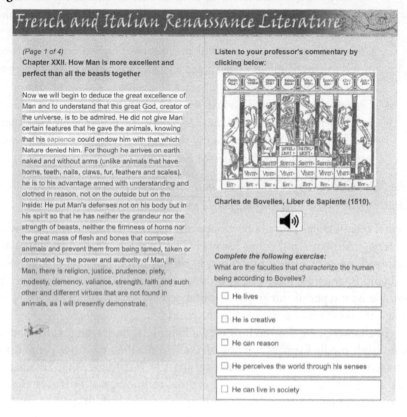

Charles de Bovelles, Liber de Sapiente (1510).

TABLE 5.2

Design Thinking Phases and Action Steps

Phase	Action Steps
Empathize	Understand the learner perspective
Define	Clearly frame the design challenge around learner needs
Ideate	Envision possible solutions
Prototype	Make the vision tangible
Test	Reality checking
Implement	The final design in action

2. *Curiosity:* This is manifested in a willingness to question the accuracy of one's own assumptions about what learners are thinking, feeling, and behaving related to a particular learning experience.

3. *Conversations:* Reaching out and making an effort to engage learners in inquisitive dialogue to get input and ideas as to what works best to achieve the desired learning outcomes.

4. *Changing or correcting:* This involves making reasonable efforts to address and remedy deficiencies in the design of a particular learning activity based on learner feedback. Taking the time to listen to and understand learner experiences is the basis for design thinking.

Use New Technology Tools and Their Affordances to Create Integrated and Impactful Learning Activities

Digital technologies provide new opportunities for learner interaction with content, instructor, and other learners. The learning design challenges are mainly about overcoming functional fixedness, using new technology tools to do old fragmented jobs. The affordances of new digital technologies make possible new types of integrated learning activities such as illustrated in the design thinking process with Professor Janus.

In chapter 3, we showed how media hybridization integrates affordances of multiple media formats and how to craft compelling narrative content for interactive case studies and scenarios using the 7Cs framework. Interactive case scenarios are just one example of how technology affordances can be used to augment conventional learning activities including case studies, stories, vignettes, role plays, and simulations. Evidence shows the effectiveness of using scenario-based learning in online environments as an engaging inductive approach for building skills and expertise (Clark, 2013).

Example Scenario-Based Learning Activity

The following is a description of a scenario-based online learning activity. Notice how the role of the learner shifts from that of a passive observer outside the case to an actual participant inside the case narrative. The learner assumes a role as the primary actor responding to realistic situations where immediate and corrective feedback can be provided in context.

> Amber teaches an undergraduate course in public health to prepare students for solving real-world problems. One of her learning activities is an online case scenario. In the scenario, learners assume the role of an intern who is working as part of an interdisciplinary team to solve a mystery disease outbreak in Bangladesh. In this scenario, learners are challenged to investigate clues related to the mystery outbreak and prevent the spread of the disease. As they engage in this activity, learners also need to learn about the culture of Bangladesh and how to work with other professionals involved in disease outbreak and prevention.

The scenario consists of a series of screens with narrative text, images of characters, photos of Bangladesh, navigation controls, and resource links. Individuals analyze situations, collect information, and make decisions requiring application of material covered in class lectures and course readings. Interviews with characters are represented with photos and speech bubbles. Maps of the outbreak, detailed disease data, interviews with local witnesses, and other project documents are also provided.

Throughout the scenario, learners are asked to make decisions and respond to questions. Decision choices are followed by consequential feedback provided by the scenario characters. One of the characters is a disease control professional (a role played by Amber) who appears at critical junctures to provide tips, feedback, and prompts for reflection. In their role as an intern, learners are asked to fill out an accompanying worksheet, where they list evidence about the cause of the disease (e.g., bacteria, fungus, and so on) and how it is transmitted to humans. In a follow-up online discussion, individuals bring their findings, discuss questions, and share experiences within their small teams. Amber connects the scenario to actual real-world events and situations and encourages personal reflection.

Scenario-based online learning activities provide a compressed, structured, and simulated experience that supports contextualization of course content and "learning-by-doing."

Integrate Multiple Learning Tasks Into an Inclusive Learning Activity

Learning activities may combine multiple tasks that integrate separate absorb-do-connect-type learning tasks into a more comprehensive and interconnected learning experience. Notice how multiple learning tasks can be tightly integrated in a learning activity in the following example:

1. The instructor provides a pedagogical wrapper to introduce the learning activity by explaining the purpose and goal, how the assigned tasks interrelate, and how the activity supports key learning objectives of the course.
2. The learner completes reading of several assigned articles, creates a summary of one selected article, and posts the summary in the group discussion forum.
3. The learner reads article summaries of other students, answers questions posted by a peer facilitator, relates learning by drawing on personal experiences, and exchanges insights with other classmates in the group discussion forum.
4. The learner creates a concept map of the interrelationships among concepts found in the articles, summaries, and discussion and shares perspectives in an open-ended group discussion. Learners reflect on each other's concept map construction and on their own learning.

5. The instructor debriefs the learning activity in the group discussion forum, highlighting key concepts and principles from the learning objectives, and how the activity ties into succeeding course units.

This integrated learning activity comprises multiple tasks. Connect-type learning tasks happen during and at the end of a discussion period. During the discussion, learners are involved in the analysis, evaluation, and synthesis of concepts through in-depth conversations. At the end of a discussion period, learners create a concept map for the readings and participate in open-ended reflections about their own learning and connection to the course topics. Concept map creation is an iterative process that allows for higher-order thinking through reflective thinking, analysis, and evaluation (Cañas et al., 2017). Sharing their concept maps with others and reflecting on their own learning moves learning to a higher-order level. Note how the instructor made explicit the interrelationship of the constituent tasks by pre-briefing and debriefing the entire learning activity.

Use Pedagogical Wrappers to Prepare Learners Cognitively and Emotionally for the Learning Activity

Well-designed online learning activities cognitively and emotionally engage learners in deep learning. One strategy for helping immerse students in a learning activity is the use of pedagogical wrappers, which we introduced in chapter 4. Pedagogical wrappers serve the following functions: (a) set the stage on both the cognitive and emotional dimensions of the learning experience at the beginning, and (b) provide closure and connection at the end of a learning activity. By making the intent explicit at the beginning of a learning activity, instructors prime learners by helping them understand the relevance and connection between the learning activity in which they are about to engage and their existing knowledge and experiences. The more complex the learning activity the greater the need for an expanded pedagogical wrapper at both the start and conclusion of the activity.

At the beginning of a challenging learning activity, learners may have different levels of prior knowledge. For learners with low prior knowledge, pedagogical wrappers can point them to targeted resources that cover prerequisite content learners need to know before engaging in the learning activity. Pedagogical wrappers can be in the form of a text or short instructor video that informs learners about what principles, techniques, or strategies they will be expected to apply during the lesson or unit and how they connect them with broader course objectives. To create emotional engagement, pedagogical wrappers should have a conversational tone as if the instructor were speaking directly with the learners. They can frame the learning activity as a compelling learning challenge rather than a compulsory task.

A pedagogical wrapper provided at the outset of an activity can help concentrate learner attention on a task, serving both a motivational and cognitive priming function. For example, if the objective for a learning activity involves an in-depth discussion, pedagogical wrappers can make the purpose of the discussion explicit and clarify the expectations, giving learners focus and sense of the activity flow. Pedagogical wrappers can disincline learners from posting surface-type messages that are explanatory, lacking problem-solving, analysis, and synthesis (Shearer et al., 2015).

For complex and more immersive types of learning activities, such as case studies, simulations, project-based learning, interactive scenarios, and games, it is helpful to have more substantial pedagogical wrappers at the beginning of a learning activity and more so at the end. At the conclusion of a learning activity, pedagogical wrappers can help to add closure and connection to the learning experience on both the cognitive and emotional dimensions. Through a debriefing summary, the instructor should make explicit the intended takeaways of the learning experience and how what they learned can be applied.

Keeping the Learner at the Center of Online Learning Activity Design

Designing engaging and impactful learning activities that are both learner and task focused is at the heart of learning experience design. Every lesson or unit in an online course should have at least one or more learning activities that challenge and engage learners in achieving higher-level learning objectives. These deep learning experiences result when the cognitive, emotional, behavioral, and social dimensions of learning are tightly integrated into an online learning activity.

Because each online course situation is different in terms of its objectives, learners, type of content, available technology, and instructional approaches, learning activities seldom come prepackaged for use. They need to be skillfully and creatively designed by adapting learning activities from other courses or crafting them anew. In this chapter, we emphasized design thinking as a mindset and approach for creating impactful and engaging learning activities that take advantage of new digital technology for the online environment. Our intention was not to prescribe, but rather to present a flexible and well-tested design process and practical strategies for adaptation to your own online course design situations.

This chapter expanded on the design of instructional content covered in chapter 4, and much of what was learned will be carried forward and expanded upon in the next two chapters related to the design of online social interactions and assessments and feedback.

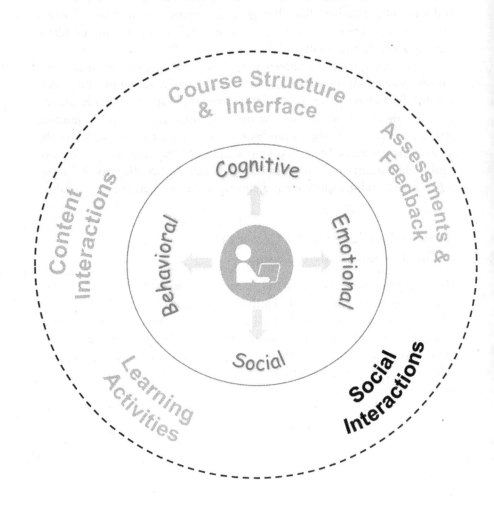

6

ENHANCING MOTIVATION, ENGAGEMENT, AND LEARNING THROUGH SOCIAL INTERACTIONS

The three common types of interactions in the online environment are learner–content, learner–instructor, and learner–learner. Chapter 4 addresses learner–content interactions. This chapter builds on learner–content interactions and focuses on the fourth design aspect: social interactions that derive from technology-mediated interpersonal communication between learner and instructor and learners with other learners. These interactions can be formal or informal via discussion forums, emails, instructor messaging, group chats, and audio or videoconferencing sessions. In the integrated framework for designing the online learning experience, social interactions enhance learner motivation, promote student engagement in active learning, and facilitate knowledge construction in a social context. The instructor plays an important role in designing and managing social interactions through actions and personalized communication that project copresence, immediacy, and intimacy. In this chapter, we explain why social interactions matter, highlight types of social interactions, identify five factors influencing the design of social interactions, provide a process for designing social interactions, and suggest strategies for integrating social interactions into learning experience design.

Guiding Design Questions

- How can a positive climate be set through social interactions?
- How can social interactions create emotional connections?

- How can personalized communication be conveyed through social interactions?
- How can learners be engaged in deep learning through social interactions?
- How can learner involvement through social interactions enhance the flow of the course?

Why Social Interactions Matter

In the face-to-face course environment, the instructor and learners are in the same space, have a clear sense of time, and are in close proximity to each other; in the online environment, it is more difficult to involve learners in social interactions. Social interactions play an essential function in learner satisfaction and persistence in online learning (Croxton, 2014). When social interactions are incorporated into an online course as a learning activity without a purpose, learners may not understand why they need to participate in a discussion or connect with other learners within the social context of the course. We have found that learners frequently view feedback from instructors in an assignment as an end in itself leading to a grade, rather than an opportunity to reflect on a higher-order learning goal in the course. Unclear course expectations, lack of clarity in direction, and poor communication from the instructor can lead to confusion, loss of focus, and feelings of disconnection on the part of learners. Instructors often overestimate learners' capacity to make connections between what is being learned in the course and their understanding of the directions provided through announcements. Learners' inability to connect with the instructor and other learners and lack of understanding of the overall goals of the course are issues that can be overcome through the intentional design of social interactions in an online course.

It has been proven that online courses with great levels of social interaction between learner and instructor and among learners point to increased levels of learner motivation, superior learning outcomes, and greater satisfaction (Park & Choi, 2009). Social interactions matter in learning experience design, but they require a shift in the course designer mindset. This involves creating personalized, engaging, and meaningful social interactions. These learning interactions can help learners recognize the purpose of the course, connect with the instructor and other learners, and increase motivation and engagement in learning experiences; however, they must be intentionally designed. Intentional design means using strategies that take into consideration the learner perspective and the learning journey throughout the course.

Strategies provide tactics to set the stage for a positive climate, create emotional connections, strengthen personalized communication, promote deep learning through learner engagement, and build learner involvement.

Types of Social Interactions

In this chapter, we focus on two types of social interactions: learner–instructor and learner–learner. These interactions may be informal or formal, synchronous or asynchronous. The right combination of learner–instructor and learner–learner interactions in online courses can enhance learner satisfaction, motivation, and achievement (Offir et al., 2008; Park & Choi, 2009) and create a memorable learning experience.

Informal social interactions may be asynchronous or synchronous. Asynchronous interactions in non-content-related forums are often used for logistical and social purposes and serve to answer logistical questions about the course, share personal and professional stories, and help with technology issues. Informal synchronous interactions may occur during virtual office hours where learners ask questions, clarify issues, or share personal experiences within the course and receive an immediate response. By including a space for informal interactions, learners can gain a sense of belonging to a learning community, helping them overcome fears about technology and find ways to express themselves in an informal manner (Conceição & Schmidt, 2010).

Formal social interactions can be accomplished during asynchronous and synchronous discussions and involve cooperative or collaborative exchanges. Learners work together in cooperative interactions to share, discuss, and synthesize ideas or concepts on a specific topic. Cooperative interactions involve content discussions or debates conducted in delayed time. Asynchronous discussion forums may be close-ended (learners answer a set of close-ended questions), open-ended (learners reflect on the learning process or develop different perspectives through open-ended questions), or integrated (including both close-ended and open-ended questions) (Ngeow & Yoon-San, 2003). In these types of formal interactions, questions may be posted by the instructor or peer facilitators. Formal synchronous discussions tend to follow the instructor presentation of content with learners located in the same virtual space or distributed into breakout rooms.

In collaborative interactions, learners work in teams to develop a product or project and complete tasks. Case studies, storytelling, and virtual team projects are examples of learning activities that include collaborative interactions (Lehman & Conceição, 2010). With videoconferencing technologies, learners engage in team tasks through synchronous interactions for same-time discussion, document sharing, and session recoding.

Formal instructor–learner interactions also include instructor communications that provide learner guidance around assignments, projects, and other learning tasks. These formal communications often include pedagogical wrappers, mentioned in chapters 4 and 5. One type of formal asynchronous instructor–learner interaction consists of a concise prefatory content message that frames the social interaction to make explicit the instructor's purpose and how a task connects with subsequent learning as well as its relationship to specific course objectives. This wrapper primes and prepares learners cognitively and motivationally before engaging in a learning task. Pedagogical wrappers can be provided by instructors in various media formats, most commonly as text, but also as audio, video, or mixed media. The instructor briefly explains the purpose of the task and the performance criteria; for more complex tasks, rubrics and worked examples can be provided. The pedagogical efficacy of simple short pedagogical wrappers at the beginning of assignments has been empirically demonstrated through transparency in the design of learning (Felten & Finley, 2019).

Instructor–learner communication, often of a less formal nature, should occur at the end of a learning unit to give a sense of closure and prepare learners for what comes next. This type of "wrap up" communication by the instructor serves to bookend a series of related assignments or a small project to ensure that learners make connections between what they have just learned and other material in the course. Although formal in purpose, these instructor–learner communications are most effective when they convey a personalized tone and style that instills a sense of instructor presence.

Both formal and informal interactions are dependent on learner motivation, engagement, and presence and are associated with all four dimensions of learning. To experience optimal learning, learners need to cognitively engage in intellectual contributions, be socially involved in the exchange of ideas with others, emotionally connect with group members, and perform meaningful tasks. Several factors influence the design of social interactions.

Factors Influencing the Design of Social Interactions

We have identified five factors that influence the learning experience when incorporating social interactions in an online course. These factors should be carefully considered to foster engagement, enhance presence, and promote learning through social interactions.

Learning Objectives Shape the Format of Social Interactions

Learning objectives are the starting point for establishing a meaningful learning experience and can shape the format of the interactions. Depending on the learning objective, the format should specify the type of interaction (learner–instructor or learner–learner), mode of communication (formal or informal), and characteristics of technology (synchronous or asynchronous). The format should align with the learning objective(s) and aid in selecting the different design aspects to incorporate into a learning interaction.

Learning objectives give a purpose for accomplishing the different social interactions within the course. For example, if the learning objectives of a course unit involve identifying, synthesizing, and reflecting on five concepts, learners may complete a set of readings (instructional content), create a concept map synthesizing the concepts (learning activity), and cooperatively participate in an open-ended discussion (social interaction) to share and reflect on the concepts.

Intimacy and Immediacy Affect Social Interactions

The online learning environment is often characterized as lacking the human element. Some of the reasons why individuals feel this way are "the lack of visual and verbal cues, doubts about the identity of those interacting with [them], and unease about feeling impersonal with others" (Lehman & Conceição, 2010, p. 14). In the face-to-face environment, intimacy is contingent on nonverbal factors such as eye contact, physical proximity, or facial expression, and immediacy is carried out through verbal and nonverbal cues. In the online environment, intimacy is achieved through the expression of emotions or feelings with others, and immediacy is based on the timing of responses. Lack of immediacy in responses during an asynchronous interaction can be frustrating to learners. Both intimacy and immediacy of social interactions are associated with the cognitive and emotional dimensions of learning.

The directness and intensity of interaction (immediacy) with the instructor can affect learning (Zhang & Oetzel, 2006). Respect, encouragement, support, and fair treatment can affect the sense of presence in learners. Immediate feedback, number of cues, language, and intent focused on the recipient can influence learners' perception of presence. When learners become aware that the instructor is copresent (intimacy) in the online environment, they perceive directness and intensity, have a close and connected relationship with the instructor, and feel present (Wei et al., 2011). Learners tend to see instructors with a high degree of online presence as positive and effective.

Technology Shapes the Context of Social Interactions

Social interactions are dependent on the social context. The social context in the online environment is based on the characteristics of the technology (synchronous or asynchronous), the learner's perceptions of the technology-mediated environment, and the online communication. Learners' perceptions of the technology include familiarity with other learners, formal and informal relationships, trust and social relationships, psychological attitude toward technology, and access and location (Sung & Mayer, 2012). Online communication is the substance that is transmitted through the medium and is the consequence of social interactions. Online communication involves the language and keyboarding skills of learners, use of icons or emoticons and paralanguage (intonation, pitch and speed of speaking, hesitation noises, gestures, and facial expression), and characteristics of synchronous and asynchronous online interactions. If a learner has a negative experience with technology or online learning prior to entering a new online course, the tendency is for the learner to enter the online environment with a negative perception of the technology-mediated social context. This affects learning and interactions with other learners.

Social Interaction Attributes Influence Learner Motivation and Engagement

The attributes of the social interactions such as types of interactions, structure of the interactions, timing of communication, group size, and interaction tasks influence learner motivation and engagement. For example, delayed communication in the online environment can be seen as forced and unnatural; learners may feel impatient while waiting for others to respond (Biesenbach-Lucas, 2003). However, some learners may find the delay in response as an opportunity to reflect before writing comments. Group discussions with more than five members can be overwhelming when the length of postings is more than one screen and group members generate multiple postings. Online synchronous interactions that mirror face-to-face lectures may not portray a feeling of personal connection. Team projects that follow a checklist for tasks may not provide a sense of flow, excitement, and accomplishment. These attributes need to be carefully considered when designing social interactions to help learners stay motivated and engaged throughout the learning experience.

Learner Characteristics Affect Social Interactions and Engagement

Age, prior knowledge, and culture and ethnicity are factors that can affect social interactions and engagement. There is a difference between how traditional-age college students and older adults perceive social interactions. Younger learners appreciate sharing their work with other learners (Walker &

Kelly, 2007); adult learners prefer to work on their own and learn what they need to learn on their own time. Prior knowledge goes in tandem with age as a factor during social interactions because prior knowledge and experience can increase engagement during online discussions when the topic is relevant and appealing. Younger learners may not have a repertoire to share in the discussion and may feel less confident engaging in social interactions.

Cultural differences play prominently in social interactions in online courses. For instance, minority students from high-context cultures tend to prefer social interactions (Ke & Kwak, 2013) and community in the online environment (Adams & Evans, 2004; Ibarra, 2000; Smith & Ayers, 2006). African American learners prefer frequent oral communication among learners, face-to-face rather than online; when taking online courses, they often want to speak to their instructors offline (Merrills, 2010). Hispanic/Latinx adult learners often demonstrate a strong preference for social interactions that are collaborative rather than competitive; the opportunity to work in groups on projects that are planned, carried out, and evaluated by the group; and reflexivity that is well supported by asynchronous discussion boards (Sanchez & Gunawardena, 1998). Because the asynchronicity feature of online learning may hinder the development of real community, it is important to intentionally design social interactions that promote engagement and explicitly encourage, coordinate, or scaffold cross-cultural online interactions.

Designing Social Interactions

One distinctive aspect of creating social interactions within the integrated framework for designing the online learning experience is the adoption of a process for designing a social interaction through the completion of tasks. These learning interactions may be preplanned or part of the emergent design during the delivery of the course. Some social interaction design may be done during the first week of the course through surveys based on learners' characteristics. Decisions about social interaction attributes such as age and prior knowledge may affect the composition of a group or team.

We suggest the following tasks for designing social interactions: establish a goal, determine the type of interaction, select the mode of interaction, identify and develop a strategy, determine the format and duration of the social interaction, define the virtual space, create expectations, and develop a course wrapper and instructor communication. Table 6.1 provides a description of the design tasks for developing social interactions. Table 6.2 shows an example of a social interaction in an online course. Table 6.3 shows expectations for group discussion of content. Figure 6.1 shows an example of a pedagogical wrapper.

TABLE 6.1
Design Tasks for Developing Social Interactions

1. Establish the goal for including social interactions within the overall purpose and objectives of the course, which include linkages and integration with other design aspects within the course.
2. Decide the type of social interaction: Learner–instructor, learner–learner, or a mix of both.
3. Select the mode of interaction: Formal or informal.
4. Identify and develop the social interaction strategy: Cooperative (debates or content discussion) or collaborative (case study, storytelling, and virtual team projects), or a mix of both.
5. Determine the format of the social interactions: Open-ended discussion, close-ended discussion, or a mix of both.
6. Determine the duration of the social interaction (e.g., number of weeks, throughout the course, beginning of a unit, end of course)
7. Define the space for the interaction: Select the technology (text, audio, video, or blend of each) and characteristics of technology (synchronous or asynchronous).
8. Create expectations. This may be done through the use of rubrics.
9. Prepare learners for the social interaction through a course wrapper and instructor communication. The course wrapper is part of the course page that describes the learning goal, requirements, guidelines, and rubric. Instructor communication invites learners to participate in the social interactions through announcements.

Strategies for Integrating Social Interactions Into Learning Experience Design

Instructors play an essential role in designing and managing social interactions in the online environment. Though the design of social interactions may seem straightforward to set up, the interpersonal interactions during the delivery of the course are unpredictable because they depend on several factors: learning objectives, intimacy and immediacy, social context, social interaction attributes, and learners' characteristics. In this book, we focus on the design aspect of social interactions, which can make it easier for the management of social interactions when delivering an online course. The design of social interactions sets the stage for a positive climate, helps create emotional connections, strengthens personalized communication, promotes deep learning through learner engagement, and builds learner involvement. The

TABLE 6.2

Example of a Social Interaction in an Online Course

Goal: The purpose is for learners to identify, analyze, and apply principles of learning experience design and the design thinking process. This activity is part of Module 2, Week 2.
Type of Social Interaction: Learner–learner.
Mode of Interaction: Formal.
Strategy: Cooperative (content discussion).
Format of the Social Interactions: Close-ended discussion. Instructor provides questions, learners respond to questions.
Duration: 2 weeks.
Space for the Interaction: Asynchronous text-based.
Expectations: Table 6.3 shows the expectations for the social interactions.
Pedagogical Wrapper: Figure 6.1 shows an example of a pedagogical wrapper.

TABLE 6.3

Expectations for Group Discussion of Content

Criterion	Description
Writing Quality	Consistently uses grammatically correct posts with rare misspellings; uses APA standards correctly
Relevance and Clarity of Post	Consistently posts topics related to the discussion; gets to the heart of the matter; expresses opinions and ideas in a clear and concise manner
Contribution to Group Learning	Answers all questions posted by the instructor; posts an initial entry on the first day and responds to others' ideas throughout the discussion; expresses ideas collegially; posts at least three substantive contributions throughout the discussion
Knowledge and Understanding of Module Topics	Demonstrates accurate understanding of the concepts and principles based on the readings; substantiates claims with evidence; shows deep critical engagement with the issues
Originality and Creativity	Explores relationships between the different concepts and principles; introduces new examples or insightful observations; attempts to develop a new or stimulating perspective on every issue

Figure 6.1. Pedagogical wrapper for a social interaction.

Module 2, Week 2: Learner Experience Design

Welcome to Module 2, Week 2! During this module, you will be able to do the following:
- Describe principles of learner-centered design
- Explain the integrated framework for designing online learning experiences
- Identify and analyze the learning experience design principles

Reading Assignments
1. Reading 1
2. Reading 2
3. Reading 3

Participate in the Discussion
After reviewing the assigned readings for this week, participate in Module 2, Week 2 Learner Experience Design discussion by reflecting on your own experience as an online learner based on what you learned from the articles.

Tips for Participating in the Group Discussion
- Be sure to provide evidence from the literature when responding to the questions.
- Each response posted must clearly tie back to the reading materials.
- You may post comments in a variety of different formats: introduce scholarly references from other sources to support or highlight perspectives; discuss personal or professional experiences.
- You may make arguments, describe experiences, or discuss alternative perspectives within the context of the reading materials. Therefore, each comment should explicitly connect with some aspect of the readings.
- Respond to at least two people in your group.

---

skillful involvement of the instructor after setting the stage will be key to establishing presence, engaging learners in the online course, and influencing intellectual curiosity (Orcutt & Dringus, 2017).

Set the Stage for a Positive Climate

Setting the course climate is a function of the instructor and it means establishing and facilitating a constructive learning environment for intellectual conversations. A positive climate sets the tone for the entire course from the get-go. Having an open and hospitable environment creates intimacy and trust between instructor and learners and among learners. Instructor actions such as getting to know learners, forming authentic relationships, building rapport with learners, and setting and reinforcing expectations are instrumental in supporting learning. Four strategies help to set the stage for a positive climate: sharing personal and professional stories, group responsibility for learning, pedagogical wrappers, and informing learners about instructor involvement.

Shared Personal and Professional Stories

Setting the tone for a positive climate can begin with the instructor's welcome video that includes a short bio, beliefs about teaching and learning, and expertise in the discipline. This may invite learners to participate in a non-content-related forum, often called "Virtual Café," during the first week of the course. In this forum, learners can share personal and professional stories and achievements through open-ended discussions. Learners may share their stories via text, audio, or video format. Learner engagement and intellectual curiosity can be influenced by the instructor's passion for the subject matter portrayed in the video or through text narratives. The video can create intimacy, a feeling that the instructor is a "real person," and encourage learner participation in the course experience. This strategy activates the social, emotional, and behavioral dimensions of learning.

Group Responsibility for Learning

Online learning demystifies the idea of the sage on the stage because the instructor and learners are in the virtual space without geographical boundaries and with a flexible concept of time. In a learner-centered environment, the course focus is on the learning experience rather than the instructor being at the center of the course. Learning is a shared responsibility between learners and instructor. Informing learners about the shared responsibility for learning is an important strategy to use in the beginning and throughout the course by using pedagogical wrappers or course announcements. Pedagogical wrappers and announcements can include explanation of expectations and guidelines for engaging in social interactions and expected engagement during social interactions before facilitated discourse. This strategy stimulates the social, cognitive, and behavioral dimensions of learning.

Pedagogical Wrappers

Creating a comfortable and secure learning environment where learners can share ideas and opinions openly and respectfully promotes deep learning. Having a protocol for communicating with others and sharing ideas about respectful and courteous postings can contribute to the trust of the online learning community (Cho & Cho, 2014). This protocol can be included in the course syllabus, lesson, or unit pages in the form of pedagogical wrappers that make explicit how to socially interact with others, emphasizing the relevance of the interaction and motivating and arousing interest in the topic.

Level of Instructor Involvement

The dominant instructor voice often displayed in face-to-face courses needs to be pulled back in the online environment. Frequency of instructor interaction can give the sense of an attentive instructor and create a positive reaction from learners (Russo & Campbell, 2004); however, instructor interactions with learners don't always increase participation in online courses; rather, overwhelming instructor involvement in online discussions can constrain learner participation (Mazzolini & Maddison, 2003). It is important to communicate to learners the level of instructor involvement in discussions, so that learners understand what is expected of them. This can influence learner engagement and motivation (Dennen et al., 2007). This strategy prepares learners to be more proactive and to become highly engaged participants in the social interactions.

Create Emotional Connections

Verbal and nonverbal cues are very important resources for creating emotional connections in a face-to-face environment. In an online course, emotional connections are created through a psychological state, an illusion formed when technology disappears and people, though separated by location, feel like they are in the same space (Lehman & Conceição, 2010). When an online learning environment has a friendly learner interface and rich media, learners are better able to share social cues with each other. The learner interface and instructor communication have significant effects on creating these emotional connections. We suggest three strategies for creating emotional connections: an intuitive learner interface, facilitative/guided communication, and logistical/organizational communication.

Intuitive Learner Interface

An online course interface that is cohesive and easily navigated, contains engaging instructional messages, and denotes an emotional tone is more likely to invite learners to interact with each other. The location, title of the discussion, description of the social interaction, and names of participants can give a sense of belonging to a group. Location within the course interface is the point of virtual gathering. This location may be part of an informal or formal interaction. The title and description of the discussion provides a sense of purpose for the social interaction. The tone of the description should encourage a sense of connection with content and other learners. The names of participants place the learning experience within a community. The social interaction environment should be intentionally designed to create a psychological sense of being present with others, reduce social distance, foster a bond among the participants, and convey friendliness within the online learning environment (Aragon, 2003).

Facilitated/Guided Communication

Facilitated and guided communication comes from the interpersonal messages of the instructor to both individuals and groups to facilitate learning. This type of communication provides coaching, mentoring, and guidance to individuals and groups and enhances learner–instructor interactions to promote engagement and deep learning. It helps create a perceptional experience at the cognitive, emotional, behavioral, and social levels. It is emergent and responsive and can be dialogic, conversational, and unstructured. It happens asynchronously during facilitated online discussion forums, synchronously during direct instruction via videoconferencing technologies, or via instructor reaction to individual and team projects. The tone of language can build up intimacy and trust through personalized comments from the instructor inviting the learner to participate in the conversation and expand insights on the topics of the discussion. The instructor's quick response to issues can prevent learner frustration and encourage ongoing participation.

Logistical/Organizational Communication

Instructor logistical and organizational communication relates to the management of the learning community and process. This type of communication provides course information, clarification of issues, instructions, and guidelines for the entire class. It can be formal and structured when addressing course netiquette, instructions for assignments, introductions to the course and parts of the course, and syllabus in text or video format as an announcement. Communication can also be informal through discussion areas where instructor and learners share personal and professional stories or during virtual office hours, usually optional, which learners attend when they have questions or want to connect with the instructor and other learners. The use of a personal and conversational tone gives a sense of caring, enthusiasm, encouragement, and presence. Ongoing communication humanizes the experience and gives a sense of being together and present with others.

Use Personalized Communication

Instructors may believe that their actions are mainly tied to cognitive (related to content) and behavioral (related to performance) engagement in the course; however, learner satisfaction is mostly connected to learners' feeling that their interpersonal communication needs are met (Dennen et al., 2007). The instructor and peers play a role in this satisfaction. Personalized communication through social greetings and acknowledgments influence learner behavior, motivation, and engagement in the course. Instructor and learners' personalized communication has a major effect in influencing learners' emotional and cognitive dimensions. Using photos or graphics, sharing beliefs and values, and acknowledging others by name make the interactions more personal, giving a sense of trust and community.

Photos or Graphics for Identifying Participants
As in social media, encouraging learners to upload their photos to their profile within the LMS can personalize the communication and give a feeling of being part of a community. Learners may also share a picture of something in their home that reflects their personality if sharing a photo is not desirable. Using graphics to convey metaphors that communicate personal characteristics can also personalize the experience.

Shared Beliefs and Values
In introductory discussions or cafés, encouraging learners to self-disclose personal stories through words can evoke emotions and feelings; this allows the instructor and learners to see each other as humans and feel a sense of being together. Learners are more likely to feel copresent if they share a kinship and have common beliefs and values with the instructor and other learners (Schimke et al., 2007). Sharing beliefs and values humanizes communication and creates personal connections. It is important to use pedagogical wrappers in social interactions to describe and evoke such feelings as part of the communication guidelines.

Acknowledging Others by Name
Learner identity is an important aspect of intimacy. Recognizing learners by name or the name of the group during discussions gives a social context for the learning experience. Expressing feelings of care and connection can lead to increased participation and social interactions (Sung & Mayer, 2012). Addressing a person by name and using salutations can help learners stay motivated and engaged with others. Encouraging intimacy and copresence through personalized communication stimulates the social and emotional dimensions of learning.

Promote Deep Learning Through Social Engagement

Instructors have the ability to influence learners' cognitive, behavioral, emotional, and social engagement in online courses. Cognitive and behavioral engagement in a course involves learners' effort, attention, and concentration on the content and involvement in the course through participation in social interactions. Emotional engagement denotes learners' excitement, curiosity, and satisfaction about a course (Cho & Cho, 2014). Social engagement involves interacting with others through interpersonal communication. All four types of engagement play an essential role in sustaining and maintaining learner motivation and engagement in deep learning in an online course. Deep learning occurs when learners use mental resources to understand complex concepts, solve problems requiring analysis and synthesis, and make decisions related to discipline-specific knowledge and experience. One example is when learners transform new information into patterned concepts and relate them to their life experiences (Wei et al., 2011). The instructor can influence deep learning through facilitated discussion, scaffolding social interactions, and use of discussion guidelines.

Instructor-Facilitated Discussion
Instructors can post challenging but manageable discussion questions or encourage learners to come up with thought-provoking questions or opinions as a way to facilitate mastery-oriented discussions (Cho & Cho, 2014). Designing challenging questions requires developing critical thinking prompts ahead of time, so that learners can elaborate, analyze, evaluate, and synthesize topics or course materials during the discussion. Learners' behaviors should include quoting from other learners' messages, referring to others' postings, asking questions, and expressing appreciation or agreement. Encouraging social engagement not only promotes deep learning but also fosters the social and cognitive dimensions of learning.

Instructor Scaffolding of Social Interactions
Scaffolding for social interactions is a way to influence learners' behavioral and emotional engagement in content interaction. It means fostering learner–instructor and learner–learner interactions that challenge thoughts in the discussion and provide feedback. For instance, facilitated questions may follow learner construction and sharing of a concept map in the discussion area through scaffolding of social interactions. Learners can review each other's concept map by comparing and contrasting the different concepts and reflecting on their learning process in the discussion area.

Discussion Guidelines
Setting guidelines for social interactions with cognitive, behavioral, and social expectations for engagement can establish the parameters for a relevant and coherent discussion. Guidelines serve as the blueprint for the

social interaction learning experience. Once established, learners understand what is expected of their cognitive, behavioral, emotional, and social engagement in the online course. Guidelines can be included in the pedagogical wrappers and as part of the rubrics for the social interaction. Although in chapter 7 rubrics are used to assess learning, in this chapter they are used as guidelines to socially engage learners in deep learning.

Build Learner Involvement Into the Flow of the Course

Learner involvement in the online course through social interactions is paramount for maintaining a successful learning experience, and it requires learners engaging behaviorally, emotionally, and cognitively to make the task more enjoyable, personalizing what is to be learned (expressing likes and dislikes, generating options), allowing for greater autonomy (sharing a preference, providing input), and gaining better access to the means for better understanding (soliciting resources, asking for assistance) (Reeve & Tseng, 2011). When learner involvement is part of the flow of the course, learners are more likely to be motivated to learn, practice self-regulation, and believe they can do the task (self-efficacy). We suggest three strategies to build learner involvement through social interactions: asynchronous free-flow areas for learner input about the course design, virtual office hours with a purpose, and debriefing at the end of the course.

Asynchronous Free-Flow Discussion

Learners' engagement in online courses can fluctuate between challenging and easy tasks. Having learners provide input, communicate a preference, present suggestions, offer a contribution, ask a question, share what they are thinking and needing, mention a goal or objective to be pursued, express their level of interest, request resources or educational opportunities, seek clarification, generate options, express likes and dislikes, or ask for assistance are examples of strategies that can be accomplished by online learners during the flow of an online course (Reeve & Tseng, 2011).

Free-flow discussion areas can be set up in a general area of the course and made available as open-ended discussion forums at the midpoint or throughout the course as a way for learners to provide formative assessment about the course through likes or dislikes and suggestions about how the course might improve. This type of learner involvement is proactive because it occurs before or during the learning activity; is intentional, making the learning opportunity more personal, interesting, challenging, or valued; and is a constructive contribution in the planning and flow of the course. Learner involvement in the flow of the course incites the emotional and behavioral dimensions of learning.

Virtual Office Hours With a Purpose
Virtual office hours are offered during scheduled times when learners can attend optional sessions with a purpose. These sessions use synchronous technologies such as videoconferencing and include a specific topic to be addressed over the course of the session. It may include clarification of a course activity, demonstration of a process, feedback on the course interface, or review of team tasks. We have found that when virtual office hours have a purpose, learners tend to attend them. The setting can use a more relaxed and personalized structure in which learners access the course site from home once a week and suggest topics and activities for subsequent meetings. This type of social interaction creates social and emotional engagement and allows learner involvement in providing feedback about the course interface, offering suggestions for relevant modifications of course structure and layout, and asking for live feedback on course tasks.

End-of-Course Debriefing
When learners are highly involved in online learning experiences, they may have a difficult time disengaging at the end of the course. This has happened in our classes and the use of an end-of-course debriefing area has helped learners reflect on their learning process, share and process feelings with classmates, and bring about closure. Courses with high involvement may create challenges in letting go of emotional connections with classmates and the instructor. A debriefing discussion area can help learners detach from the course and move out of the flow.

Social Interactions for Learning Experience Design

Social interactions can serve as the medium for keeping learners motivated and intellectually curious to learn, emotionally connected and engaged in the course, and actively participating in the design and flow of the course. Social interactions are influenced by learning objectives, intimacy and immediacy, technology-mediated social context, social interaction attributes, and learner characteristics. Social interactions in the online environment depend on the copresence of all involved and must be intentionally designed to create memorable learning experiences. In this chapter, we have provided a process for designing social interactions and have suggested strategies for integrating social interactions into learning experience design. The instructor plays an important role in designing and managing social interactions. Setting the stage for a positive climate, creating emotional connections, using personalized communication, promoting deep learning, and building learner involvement into the course flow are strategies that help enhance learner motivation, engagement, and learning through social interactions.

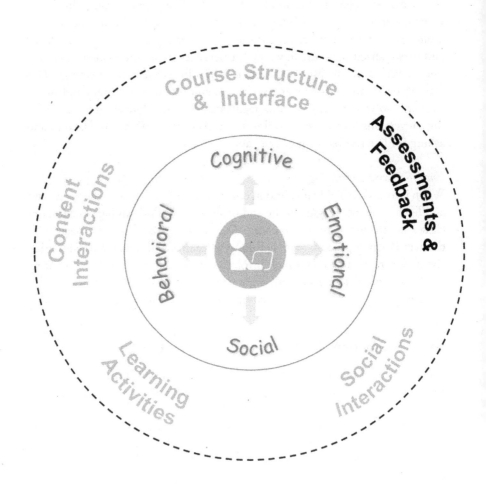

INCORPORATING ASSESSMENTS AND FEEDBACK THROUGHOUT THE LEARNING EXPERIENCE

The last design aspect, assessments and feedback, is paramount for creating an impactful learning experience. Most assessment strategies focus on a specific topic and point in time during the course without connecting to the entire learning experience. For example, students read course content, participate in learning activities, and complete assessments as fragmented, linear, or separate events. It is important to look at assessments and feedback as learning experiences integrated into the entire course as students go in and out of flow throughout their course journey. In the integrated framework for designing the online learning experience, assessments and feedback focus on the learner perspective first and foremost, are intentionally incorporated into the entire learning experience during the course design, create flow and engagement, monitor student self-knowledge, leverage learner confidence, sustain learner motivation, and integrate learner agency. In this chapter, we explain the differences between assessments and feedback, provide ways for rethinking assessments and feedback as learning experiences, and provide strategies for incorporating assessments and feedback into learning experience design.

Guiding Design Questions

- How can we better design assessments and feedback considering stages of learner development and prior learning?
- How can we incorporate assessments throughout the online learning experience?

- How can we design assessment activities to be more engaging and conducive to deep learning experiences?
- How can we use assessments and feedback to establish and sustain learner attention and motivation?
- How can we design assessments that help learners monitor their own learning?

Differences Between Assessments and Feedback

In this book, we refer to *assessments* as strategies used to evaluate learners' content knowledge, demonstration of a skill or task, development of a product, or experience of a process. Assessments can be conducted at the start of a course when learners enter the online environment as a way to obtain information about learners' prior knowledge and throughout the course to determine if learners are acquiring knowledge or skills as evidence of learning progress. This type of assessment is formative, and the main purpose is to improve learning and provide information about learner development. Assessments at the end of the course are summative and they determine if learners met the course outcomes. Learning assessments are often connected to a rubric, standards, grade, or a badge. Although assessments of learning assignments are graded and feedback is not included in conventional design practices, we suggest assessments and feedback to be used interwoven with each other in order to create flow and impact learning.

Feedback is best described by Fink (2013) as "a dialogue with the learner" (p. 105). This dialogue may be between the learner and the content, the learner and the activity, the learner and the instructor, or among the learners with each other. Molloy and Boud (2014) said that feedback "acts like a mirror, to reflect back to the learner 'what their performances look like'" (p. 414). Though learners often view assessments as feedback, we should look at feedback as a system of learning instead of discrete episodes of instructors telling students about their performance. This perspective focuses on the premise that assessments and feedback as a design aspect are part of a process that sustains learner attention and motivation.

In this book, we move away from blocked assessments that test students on a specific topic infrequently (e.g., a midterm or a final exam). Blocked assessments are fragmented, linear, and decontextualized. Fragmentation means breaking assessments into separate episodes without connecting them into the entire course experience. In an online environment, assessments are often arranged in a linear order of events such as read content, participate in learning activities, and complete assessments. This order works like a checklist without creating flow. *Decontextualized* means placing assessments in isolation from the context of the learning experience in the course. Our goal is to give greater emphasis to thinking, feeling, doing, and relating to others when creating assessments. Feedback is reframed as coaching in which learners are shown what they know and how they can do things better. This approach is learner-centered and holistic and takes advantage of new technologies and digital pedagogies. Technologies provide the means to create flow and connect design aspects with each other.

Rethinking Assessments and Feedback as Learning Experiences

Assessments and feedback can have an impact on online learning success and student motivation. Lee (2014) found that online student satisfaction is closely related to explicit course expectations, clear guidelines on assignments, rubrics, and constructive feedback; however, these factors are often addressed as separate components in course design, rather than being contextualized as part of the entire learning experience.

Encouraging students to view assessments as engaging activities from which they can learn and grow rather than terminal judgments about themselves can be a challenge. Students tend to be assessment-focused, view assessment as a checklist leading to a grade, and expect to see the relevance of the learning activity to achieving their desired goals. Learning activities that are relevant and closely paired with assessments can motivate learners to engage with content and other course activities (Rogerson-Revell, 2015).

Rethinking assessments and feedback as learning activities involves moving away from functional fixedness. We suggest integrating assessments and feedback into the learning experience with the purpose of creating flow and engagement, monitoring learner self-knowledge, leveraging learner experience, sustaining learner motivation, and encouraging learner agency.

Spacing and Interleaving Assessments to Create Flow and Engagement

McCracken et al. (2012) talked about designing assessments as a sequence of events developed early on in the design process and aligned with the learning activities and outcomes. These events need to be integrated and connected with the design aspects and incorporated into the holistic learning experience. For example, spacing and interleaving (alternating) assessments between content presentations and learning activities or embedding assessments and connecting them to new learning can help students create relevant associations within content (Miller, 2014), maintain flow, and sustain engagement as the course progresses. Spacing and interleaving provide a way to alternate topics and work on several related skills together instead of working one at a time. This approach may be more difficult for initial learning, but it pays off in long-term retention because learners circle back to previously exposed content (Roediger & Pyc, 2012).

Flow has been described as a holistic sensation of total involvement, a state when a person performing an activity is totally engaged in the activity. Pearce et al. (2005) proposed that flow can be a process rather than a state. Students may go in and out of flow throughout a task performance depending on the learner's skill and how challenging the task is. Sometimes students are not ready to learn a topic. Low-stakes assessments, such as short quizzes, spaced in-between topics, can provide students with feedback about their performance and where they need improvement. Low-stakes assessments can provide an opportunity for students to review the materials and retake the quiz. This type of assessment is formative and allows for further learning about the topic.

Using Learner Self-Assessment as a Tool to Monitor Self-Knowledge

One strategy to use formative assessments is to ask students to self-assess their missteps in the test by reflecting what was done wrong and why and ask them to figure out how to make it better. This approach allows students to learn from mistakes and make judgments about their own performance. In this case, learners are at the center of the process and monitor their own learning (Molloy & Boud, 2014). This encourages self-knowledge and self-regulated learning, which impacts motivation for learning and performance.

In our integrated framework for designing the online learning experience, self-knowledge plays an important role in learning, because it can help to facilitate deep learning in students (Crisp, 2012). When students' self-knowledge is aligned with metacognitive awareness, they are more likely to appreciate what they do not understand and their ability to connect approaches to learning to unfamiliar situations (Wiggins et al., 2005), creating a more meaningful learning experience.

Self-assessment has been shown to have a positive influence on students' self-regulated learning and self-efficacy. It can increase self-regulatory actions related to learning goals when students monitor their own progress and evaluate and correct for errors. By taking control of their own learning and believing they can succeed on a task, students may also experience less fear of failure (Panadero et al., 2017).

Leveraging Learner Competence Through Instructor Feedback

Instructor feedback has an influence in student self-assessments because students can overestimate their metacognitive abilities to self-assess objectively.

This overestimation of one's memory performance, also called illusions of competence, are held disproportionately when learners have high expectations about their performance (Koriat & Bjork, 2005). Therefore, instructor feedback can help students leverage their competence.

Also, there is a tendency for learners to have optimistic and miscalibrated perspectives about themselves when facing difficult tasks (Kruger & Dunning, 1999). *Calibration* is "a measure of the relationship between confidence in performance and accuracy of performance (Stone, 2000, p. 437). Instructor feedback can help learners expand knowledge and align confidence to match the learning reality. Instructor response to task performance can provide students tactics for improving their level of competence on a given subject or skill.

Instructor feedback is an opportunity to reinforce a growth mindset for learners. Students with a fixed mindset are only interested in knowing if they are right or wrong, if they passed or failed a test. Conversely, students with a growth mindset are interested in feedback that expands their knowledge and abilities; they gain from their mistakes and feedback (Dweck, 2006). A growth mindset requires time and effort on the part of learners, resulting in increased motivation and achievement. How feedback is provided can impact student motivation and growth in a course. Feedback directed at the process encourages a growth mindset; feedback directed at the person or outcomes can be negative and does not motivate learning.

Sustaining Learner Motivation Through Timing, Language, and Type of Feedback

Timing of feedback can have an effect on learners' motivation and performance. Timing is related to frequency (regularly, consistently, and promptly). Regular feedback is ongoing throughout the course and helps learners to feel their work is recognized; consistent feedback is provided on a constant pace and gives self-confidence to learners. Prompt feedback is provided immediately after an assignment, a task, or a process. Learners feel feedback is most effective when it is provided immediately after task engagement because it solidifies their learning and guides understanding of concepts (Lehman & Conceição, 2014); however, delaying feedback on complex tasks may help learners reflect on the process (Molloy & Boud, 2014).

The language (or tone) of feedback can affect student performance and motivation too. The following five common types of feedback related to tone and language have been shown to be effective: praise, encouragement, recognition of insightful learning, constructive criticism, and rewards. In a study of teachers and students in the online environment, Lehman and Conceição

(2014) found that positive reinforcement worked as praise and encouragement for students to feel confident and motivated to persevere in the course; recognition of learners' progress assisted students in becoming aware of their learning development; constructive criticism provided insights on students' progress and helped them stay motivated to expand their learning. Using an optimistic tone during constructive criticism can impact learners' performance positively. For students who focus on rewards for going above and beyond assigned work, bonus points, extra credit, or assignment waivers can also reinforce motivation and a sense of accomplishment for students. Feedback can have implications for the cognitive and emotional dimensions of learning. When empathy, understanding, and care are part of the feedback message, students are likely to feel good and accomplished.

Digital technologies can help enhance instructor feedback and impact student learning and motivation. For the most part, instructors use text commentary when providing feedback in online courses; however, with the propagation of inexpensive digital technologies, it has become common for instructors to use rich media to provide learner feedback. Orlando (2016) has conducted a study comparing text, voice, and screen-casting feedback to online students. Students perceive that they retain content better when they receive voice feedback rather than text feedback. Also, voice feedback gives a better sense of instructor caring because the tone of voice gives a personal touch and sense of presence.

From an instructor perspective, voice feedback may be more efficient because it takes less time to record than writing a text comment. Voice feedback also allows learners to understand nuance, because it is difficult to express emotions in text format. For students, instructor voice feedback shows empathy and makes the online environment less lonely and more motivating; feedback is more in-depth because the instructor gives advice and is more encompassing of global issues with the focus on the content rather than the writing. An enhancement to voice feedback is screen-casting—video screen capture containing audio narration. Screen-casting has been shown to be a favorite for instructors compared to text feedback because it is more personal and creates a better emotional connection with students.

Digital technology can provide benefits for the quantity and quality of instructor feedback, but it depends on the course context, learner characteristics, and technology used in the course. LMSs now have the capability to use text, voice, and screen-casting for instructor feedback. It requires instructor technology training, understanding learners' needs, and matching the technology to the context of the course. Providing voice feedback on a long paper may not meet the needs of learners because the learner will be able to connect the feedback only if the paper is viewable on the screen; thus, in this case the text format or screen-casting may be more appropriate so that the learner can view the paper and hear the instructor voice feedback. For instructor feedback that explains the process and requires nuances, voice feedback may be more appropriate. Feedback that requires demonstrating a process or a procedure may benefit from screen-casting.

Integrating Learner Agency Into Assessments and Feedback

In the integrated framework, assessments and feedback work together and can equally impact student learning and should emphasize that the learner is the one with agency who constructs knowledge rather than the one who gains knowledge (Molloy & Boud, 2014). Therefore, it is important to rethink assessments and feedback in terms of the learner perspective using the four dimensions of learning.

From a cognitive perspective, assessments and feedback should be detailed to promote meaningful and impactful learning, build on previous learning in the course, encourage growth and development, and challenge and prompt learners to do more thinking about their own learning. From an emotional perspective, feedback should be encouraging and affirming to build self-confidence, timely so that students are motivated to learn, and conversational to create a sense of ease. From a behavioral perspective, assessments and feedback should encourage students to try new strategies, persist in the face of challenging tasks, and be an active contributor to the course design by reacting to the environment and providing input about changes. From a social perspective, assessments and feedback are about interacting and communicating with others in groups or teams and with the instructor and enabling feelings of understanding and sense of presence. When learners are given ownership of their own learning and feel they are active contributors to the learning environment by providing feedback, they will invest more, be more motivated, and show more interest in the task.

Incorporating Assessments and Feedback Into Learning Experience Design

Assessments and feedback can guide students in constructing, connecting, and applying knowledge. Certain assessment strategies combined with feedback at different points of the course can provoke curiosity, create self-awareness of one's own learning, stimulate engagement with content and peers, and promote deep learning. Keeping in mind the four dimensions of learning, assessments and feedback are not mere fragmented approaches to evaluate student learning; rather, they should be integrated with content interactions, learning activities, and social interactions to create optimal learning experiences. We suggest strategies for integrating assessments and feedback into the course design next.

Design Assessments and Feedback Based on a Learner Growth Mindset

Instructors and course designers are inclined to create assessments from an instructional perspective without taking into account stages of learner development and prior knowledge. Learner-centered design means looking at assessments and feedback from the learner perspective. Assessments that place the learner at the center of the task are more likely to meet the mental, emotional, behavioral, and social needs of the learner. To help learners shift their mindset about assessments and feedback, instructor messages in the form of pedagogical wrappers can explain the goal of the activity and how learners will gain from feedback received by the instructor.

Pedagogical wrappers explaining the purpose and goal of the activity can help learners think of assessments and feedback as a strategy to expand their knowledge and abilities and learn from their mistakes, a chance to grow and develop. Encouraging learners to focus primarily on their learning process, rather than the product (final grade), should be intentionally designed. Feedback should stimulate thinking, feeling, doing, and relating with others as part of the learning experience.

Incorporate Emotional and Cognitive Elements Into Assessments and Feedback to Infuse Interest, Challenge, and Curiosity

Incorporating emotions such as confusion, frustration, anxiety, challenge, delight, and surprise during the learning activity are more likely to promote deep learning, challenge learners' thinking, and infuse curiosity to continue to learn, but they are more effective if assessments and feedback strategies are intentionally incorporated into the activity. We provide a few examples of learning activities and how to incorporate emotional and cognitive elements into assessments and feedback.

Concept Mapping

Concept mapping is an activity that requires learners' construction of knowledge through the creation of a graphic representation of personal meaning, an external representation of schemas and structural knowledge (Jonassen et al., 1997). Building a concept map requires learners to identify concepts in a discipline-specific content area and relate these concepts with each other through concept hierarchy, propositions, and cross-links. Assessments can include a rubric that delineates the concepts and terminologies indicating reorganization of learners' cognitive structure, changes of cognitive structure through relationships among concepts, and ability to communicate understanding through the graphic representation.

When concept mapping, learners can acquire new knowledge by connecting to previous knowledge already in their memory, which is much easier for the mind to retrieve. Creating a concept map, learners have the ability to create many connections between new ideas and previous knowledge by restructuring knowledge and permanently positioning the new knowledge into their long-term memory. This activity is learner-centered and has cognitive elements that can infuse interest, challenge, and curiosity because it is about learners' mental representation of their own knowledge. Although having students create a concept map can be viewed as a separate learning activity, it is best to nest it within other design aspects. For instance, learners first complete several content reading assignments (content interaction), which might conclude with a discussion forum session with peers (social interaction). Next, they create concept maps followed by instructor corrective feedback (assessment). The instructor feedback focuses on misrepresentations of knowledge.

Virtual Team Project

This activity can create feelings of excitement, anxiety, frustration, and accomplishment when students are involved in the creation of a product or involved in a process. During the team process, incorporating assessment opportunities in the form of self-reflections at different stages can help students focus on the learning process rather than primarily on product creation. Assessment questions focus on perceptions of their learning by sharing feelings and milestones during the formative stages of the work and giving a sense of accomplishment. Self-reflection can provoke awareness of the emotional and social dynamics of the team and help members rethink strategies for a more effective and efficient process. Instructor feedback should involve encouragement and acknowledgment of team accomplishments or monitoring of progress. It is important for the instructor to avoid prescribing the team process, so that students reflect on their learning process.

Asynchronous Online Group Discussions

Asynchronous online group discussions may be done in a group setting, but students may view the activity as an individual graded assignment. Group activities in which students focus only on responding to the assignment meet the cognitive dimension but lack the emotional connection among group members. Group discussions that are set up with role assignments can help build an emotional element into the activity by building group trust and creating social presence. Cognitive elements (e.g., concept relevance, clarity, and understanding) can be easily infused into assessment strategies through a. rubric; however, the emotional elements are often left out. Emotional elements can be incorporated into the rubric through contribution to group learning by focusing on collaboration, collegiality, open communication, group cohesion, personal perspective, and emotional expressions. Instructor immediate and regular feedback on the activity can remind students of their contributions to group learning and encourage interest and cooperation.

Embed Assessments and Feedback Into the Learning Experience to Promote Engagement and Deep Learning

Stealth assessments involve embedding formative assessments into the online learning environment. This type of assessment is invisible and does not disturb learning and engagement and may alternate between topics and have different purposes: improve student learning, promote student self-efficacy, offer timely feedback, provide information at different levels of the learning process, furnish low-to-mid-stakes assessments, and use developmental models (Shute & Kim, 2014). Stealth assessments require an integrated approach for bringing together design aspects to create a holistic learning experience. Using digital technologies, assessments can be easily embedded into content interactions, learning activities, and social interactions. Examples of learning activities that can embed assessments and feedback to promote engagement and deep learning include quizzes, case scenarios, problem-based learning, and gamified assessments.

Quizzes

Quizzes can be embedded easily into content interactions, learning activities, and social interactions. Orientations are usually included in the beginning of the course. Instructors like to gather learner characteristics and prior knowledge during orientation activities; quizzes can be used as a preassessment tool to identify gaps in student knowledge. To test understanding of concepts, quizzes can be embedded immediately after content interactions as learning aids for future retention of knowledge. Quizzes may also be used to help organize information in categories at certain points in the interaction with content to allow better retrieval. When the goal is for learners to apply knowledge to new contexts, quizzes can be embedded using a case example with complex questions evoking decision-making. Quizzes may also be embedded as a self-assessment of knowledge to enhance metacognitive awareness (Roediger et al., 2011). Embedded assessments in a quiz format can be best used as disguised knowledge checks interwoven between content presentations to engage learners with the content and encourage deep learning.

Scenario-Based Activities

Scenario-based learning activities include story-like narratives of authentic situations likely to be encountered in real-world professional practice. New digital tools enable instructors to craft interactive media-rich scenarios delivered online where individual learners are called on to apply discipline-specific knowledge and skills. Interactive scenarios can function as assessment tools that include critical decision points (in the narrative) where learners are called on to make informed choices demonstrating their application of course content. Using software applications, consequential feedback can also be included in scenarios. Scenario-based learning assessments typically have a story-like look and feel, with contextualized assessment questions framed around real-world challenges. Because of this, they have the potential to engage learners at deeper cognitive and emotional levels compared to traditional assessment formats. Scenarios can present knowledge application questions with multiple acceptable answers, where learners must not only describe their responses but also justify them. In this circumstance, rubrics may be needed to establish criteria for assessment purposes. A blended assessment approach incorporating scenarios can also be used. For example, factual and conceptual knowledge can be assessed through conventional quiz questions followed by a scenario that assesses application of principles, mental models, or problem-solving strategies (Clark, 2013).

Problem-Based Learning

Embedded assessment can be incorporated into problem-based learning activities for understanding and knowledge application (Jonassen, 2014). If the goal of the activity is deep learning, ill-structured problems tend to be more complex. Students can construct a response or a product. The use of a rubric to describe performance provides evidence of competence. Another approach for problem-based learning is when students construct the problems and have control of the context. The complexity of the problem has implications for working memory requirements and comprehension. Complex problems impose more cognitive load on the learner. Instead of viewing the assessment as a knowledge test, embedding assessments like quizzes to check on knowledge application can create excitement for solving the problem, which promotes engagement in the activity and ultimately involves the learner in deep learning.

Gamified Assessment

According to Kapp et al. (2014), *gamification* is "using game-based mechanics, aesthetics, and game-thinking to engage people, motivate action, promote learning, and solve problems" (p. 54). It does not mean that an instructor or course designer must create a game for the course; rather, they create activities that feel like a game. There are two types of gamification: structural and content. Structural gamification applies game elements but does not modify content; the structure around the content is designed based on a game format, but it is not a game. Through stories using characters, students can solve problems by achieving different levels of accomplishment. The content in this format motivates learners through the use of rewards such as badges, achievements, or levels of accomplishment. Content gamification is more like a game; it uses challenges to engage learners in the context; it involves some action to motivate learners to complete an activity. One example of game-like activity is when learners are challenged to an activity that goes throughout the course; they receive badges after completing different levels of accomplishments. The activity builds on skills and promotes deep learning.

Involve Learners in Assessments and Feedback to Spark Interest and Sustain Motivation

Conventional design practices develop assessments from the instructor perspective. It is an individual process in which the instructor determines the criteria, standards, and format or assessment activities. In this case, students are not involved in design decisions. When the course is designed in collaboration with other stakeholders, the course will more closely meet the learning needs of students. Involving learners in continuous participatory design can be accomplished during the course as part of a learning activity in which learners create assessment strategies during projects or through learner feedback on course design as touch points during the course to check how the course design is working for all.

Assessments Created by Learners

Student involvement in assessment creation can be incorporated into team projects or self-directed learning activities. An example of a learner assessment creation involves a team project in which students create questions for a product review. Questions are initially used for a prototype review and then later for a product review. Student involvement in assessment creation is particular to the project and requires students to think more globally. A common self-directed learning activity involving learner assessment-building is a learning contract. A learning contract is an agreement negotiated between a learner and the instructor identifying the goals and activities of a specific task or an entire course. Students create the goals, activities, assessments, and evidence of accomplishments. These two types of assessment created by learners give them power to take the initiative to identify their own activities and assessments and can spark interest in accomplishing tasks. The instructor role is to monitor student development, growth, and achievements through constructive feedback and recognition of student work.

Learner Feedback on Course Design

Formative feedback on course design can play an important function in sustaining student motivation. Feedback can be obtained weekly during virtual office hours with a purpose or midsemester evaluations in the form of surveys asking questions that convey feelings and perceptions of the learning environment and course activities. Virtual office hours can start with an open discussion about the course interface and structure, examination of technology features, and assignment expectations. Then, move to a more specific focus on assignments to check for student understanding of concepts. Students feel good when they have something to say about modifying the online learning environment. Participatory design gives learners agency and uses a feedforward approach, the ability to know ahead of time if the course is on track. When learners are involved in the design process through feedback, they are more invested, motivated, and interested in the learning process.

Include Iterative Self-Assessment Approaches to Encourage Self-Regulated Learning

Online learning is an iterative phenomenon and requires strong time management skills, self-motivation, and self-regulation. A course that includes self-assessments as part of the iterative learning process helps students control the pace of their learning and has a positive effect on students' self-regulated learning and self-efficacy (Panadero et al., 2017). Self-assessments can help learners become aware of their learning goals and how to monitor and evaluate their own performance. Self-assessments can be incorporated immediately after a task as a reflection of one's personal learning process or accomplished upon receiving instructor feedback to reflect on errors and ways to resolve mistakes.

Self-Assessment Immediately After a Task

One example of a self-assessment conducted after a task is when students construct concept maps and self-assess their learning immediately after completing the task. This self-assessment includes reflecting on relationships among concepts not seen before, easiest relationships among concepts depicted, most difficult relationships depicted, and reasons these relationships were easy or hard to depict. Further reflection includes looking at the concept map and thinking back on the online discussion and reflecting if there were relationships between the concepts read and the online discussions, moments in the online discussion students felt disoriented or confused and, if so, whether the construction of the concept map provided any clues about why they felt this way. These iterative self-reflections based on students' perceptions and attitudes toward their individual construction of knowledge allow students to refine and expand their knowledge and construct personal meaning (Conceição et al., 2009). Often students redo their concept maps after the self-reflections because the self-assessment of their own work elicited change in their learning. By cycling back through self-reflections of their learning process, students expand their knowledge and increase their self-regulatory actions.

Self-Assessment Upon Receiving Instructor Feedback
Another example of iterative self-assessment is when students receive feedback on an assignment and the instructor allows students to reflect on components of the assessment that contained errors, provide new solutions for the errors by stating what was incorrect, or state how the solution can be solved in a different way. This type of self-assessment allows students to learn from mistakes and is iterative because the learner loops back into what they did and evaluates their own performance. It gives learners a second chance for looking at their own work, promotes self-efficacy (Panadero et al., 2017), and helps with metacognitive awareness and tuning of schemas.

Exploring New Approaches for Assessments and Feedback

Assessments and feedback best meet mental, emotional, behavioral, and social learning needs if they are designed from a learner perspective as part of the entire learning experience. Students who focus on assessments and feedback as part of their holistic experience will be more motivated and engaged with content and other course activities. This requires a shift in students' mindset. Instructors and course designers who intentionally integrate assessments and feedback need to focus on creating flow and engagement, monitoring learner self-knowledge, leveraging learner experience, sustaining learner motivation, and encouraging learner agency. Spacing and interleaving assessments within content interactions, learning activities, and social interactions can create flow and engagement and ultimately promote deep learning experiences. Involving learners in assessments and feedback can spark interest and sustain learners' attention and motivation. When exploring and developing new approaches, instructors and course designers need to consider new digital technologies and pedagogies as resources for enhancing the quality of online assessments and feedback strategies.

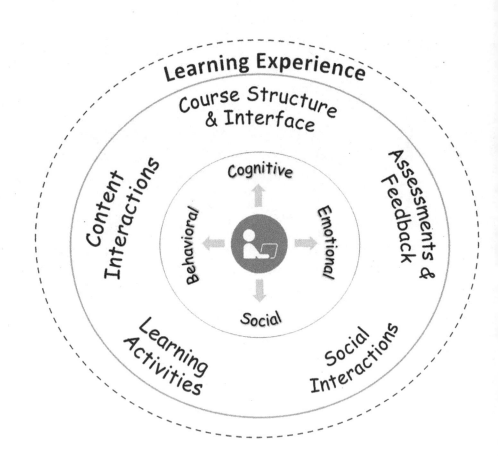

8

PUTTING IT TOGETHER

Using the integrated framework for designing the online learning experience may seem overwhelming, with so many concepts, design aspects, principles, and strategies to be put together holistically. In this chapter, we provide an example illustrating a real-world application of the principles and strategies covered in the book using design thinking to create learning experiences. We also provide a summary of the guiding design questions and design strategies for each design aspect in the integrated framework. We conclude with approaches for moving forward in designing the online learning experience.

Using Design Thinking for Creating Learning Experiences

We illustrate the use of design thinking for creating integrated learning experiences. Design thinking includes five phases: empathize with learners, define the learners' needs, create ideas for innovative solutions, prototype, and test.

Empathize With Learners

Empathizing with learners is the foundation of learner-centered and learner experience design. To empathize is to put oneself into the place of the learner who will be interacting with the instructional material or learning tasks. Understanding the perspective of learners is a way to overcome the natural tendency to use oneself as the point of reference and recognize that learners likely do not approach and react to a learning experience like a course designer may assume. Empathy is less about compassion and more about genuine curiosity and interest in the learner experience and a desire to make it better. Establishing empathy requires direct in-person conversations with learners, asking questions, and listening to them to better understand their perspective. This can be done informally and quickly through brief interviews with learners. These insights enable course designers to craft experiences that address learner needs from the cognitive, emotional, behavioral, and social dimensions of learning.

Interview Learners
Whether you are creating the course for the first time or converting a face-to-face course to the online environment, interview learners to understand the course's audience, purpose, and content. If you are enhancing an existing course, look at your previous course evaluations and talk with students who took your course earlier. The intent of the interview is to gain first-hand experience in understanding learner goals, motivations, and behaviors associated with the course. Construct questions to uncover emotions that support learning for your interviewees. Figure 8.1 provides tips for conducting interviews.

Define Learners' Needs

Synthesizing insights gained about learners through empathizing enables course designers to create a more accurate mental picture of learners and how they think, feel, and react to a particular learning situation. This imaginary mental profile of learners is often referred to as a *learner persona*. The purpose of the define phase is to use these personas to articulate and frame the design goal and challenges in a learner-centered way. In this phase, synthesize the interviews or conversations, create a learner persona, and provide problem statements.

Synthesize Interviews
Synthesizing interviews will help identify patterns around common behaviors, goals, and concerns about the course. These patterns will help identify opportunity areas and envision an ideal learning experience. They should include patterns found in the interviews—challenges, surprising insights, and strengths of the course.

Create a Learner Persona
After analyzing the patterns identified from the interviews, create a learner persona that portrays a learner in the course. The persona should represent a composite of the patterns across *all* interviews. It should *not* represent a single person. The learner persona should show how learners think, feel, and react to learning in your online course.

Figure 8.1. Tips for conducting interviews.

- Ask why, even if you think you know the answer. Don't assume you know what users are thinking or feeling—sometimes, their answers might surprise you.
- When probing their experiences in the course, ask for positive and negative incidents that impacted their learning.
- Avoid close-ended questions. These questions can be answered with "yes" or "no" or another simple phrase.
- Use open-ended questions to encourage storytelling. Example stem phrases include the following:
  - "How do you . . . ?"
  - "What is it like to . . . ?"
  - "Why do you feel . . . ?"
  - "Can you tell me about a time when . . . ?"
- Organize the questions into the three phases:
  - *Phase One: Set the stage.* Make a personal connection.
    - Tell me a little bit about yourself.
    - How do you like to spend your time?
  - *Phase Two: Capture stories.* Go deep on one or two stories.
    - Tell me when you took the course.
    - Why did you take the course?
    - Were there any issues with the course? Tell me more.
    Probe: activities, challenges, and emotions.
  - *Phase Three: Finish on a high note.*
    - What makes for a really great course experience?
    - If you had a tip or piece of advice for someone taking this course, what would you tell them?

Source. Adapted from Interaction Design Foundation. (n.d.). *Conducting interviews with empathy.* https://public-media.interaction-design.org/pdf/Conducting-an-Interview-with-Empathy.pdf

Provide Problem Statements

Being able to articulate the design challenges focused around learner characteristics guides and sharpens design efforts moving forward. The information from the learner persona should provide clues to the course design challenges and help you create problem statements. The problem statements provide a clear vision or goal for the course design.

Create problem statements by framing your ideas through "How might we?" questions. Adapt questions to allow for a variety of solutions. "How might we?" questions should generate a number of possible answers. If your questions are too broad, narrow them down. Design challenge definitions are typically stated in a "How can we?" format and are solution-agnostic. The following are examples of definition statements related to the design:

- How can we get learners emotionally engaged in this task so that they seek out additional content from the ___ and ___?
- How can we get learners to immediately apply the concepts in the tutorial to a real-life challenging problem?

The problem statements should incorporate learner needs as actionable problems that will drive the aspects of the course design. Frame the problems as insightful, actionable, unique, narrow, meaningful, and exciting statements. Consider using the following structure to write your problem statements:

> _____ needs to _____ because _____
> [Learner]   [leaner's needs]   [insights]

Create Ideas for Innovative Solutions (Ideate)

After developing a clear and comprehensive definition of the learning design goal and challenge, productively generate ideas and approaches to address them. The main focus of the ideate phase is to envision possibilities regarding both the learning goals and learner needs and characteristics. One does not do this alone, and it requires enlisting a few colleagues and learners who understand the challenge to participate in brainstorming. This does not necessarily have to take place at a single instance in time in a meeting room with lots of flip charts in whiteboards. It could be done over an extended period of time over a few meetings.

When brainstorming a range of ideas, it is better to defer judgement on evaluating those ideas and avoid embracing the first seemingly good idea. One unique caveat for ideation in the context of online learning design is possessing at least some understanding of the range of affordances of available technology tools and software but not becoming constrained by them. Involving a learning technologist in the process is most helpful. Ideation is best facilitated by having participants frame ideas in a positive way in the form of "What if?" statements:

- What if the learning activity had elements that felt like a treasure hunt, and clues were to be found in a variety of online resources including YouTube videos?

- What if the introductory text material in the learning activity included a short case scenario with virtual characters with whom learners interact to solve a set of problems related to key concepts?

Ideation often starts with a cloudy idea about how the learning experience should work. Over time ideas begin to crystallize into a more clear and complete image. This usually involves some sketches and models that bring the cloudy idea into a more tangible and concrete form. Words describe the idea and then get translated into pictures or drawings. These then gradually transition into the next phase of prototyping the best ideas.

Prototype

This phase involves taking two or three of the best ideas generated during the ideation phase and putting them into a tangible form. This is often referred to as rapid prototyping. At this phase, candid ideas are translated into a more tangible and concrete form, often crude but something that can be visualized to show others for feedback. In this phase, you create a prototype, obtain feedback, and analyze the feedback.

A prototype is a first draft of an idea or rough mockup of a design solution that course designers test out with real people. Minimal time and resource investment are used to produce a prototype. The best prototyping tool is simply hand drawn sketches using a pencil and paper or a whiteboard. Prototypes should be regarded as throwaways; course designers should be able to easily let go of ideas that don't seem to be meeting all of the criteria. During this stage, iteration is a common action. Prototypes need to be tweaked and refined rapidly and easily. Prototypes should be shown to other people to get initial reactions and feedback.

Identify a learning experience based on a course objective involving multiple design aspects to prototype. For example, you may create a learning experience connected to a higher-order learning objective (complete a pathology analysis):

1. Watch a video with a professional demonstrating how to perform a particular procedure (learner–content interaction)
2. Study a manual regarding policies and procedures for conducting a pathology test (learner–content interaction)
3. Check your knowledge quiz (assessment)
4. Analyze speech patterns using a simulation (learning activity)
5. Complete a form analyzing a patient speech pattern (assessment)

Create Sketches, Models, Scenarios, or Storyboards
Create a prototype of the learning experience using sketches, models, scenarios, or storyboards showing the interconnections of the multiple design aspects. For example, for the video, create a storyboard. For the manual, create a pedagogical wrapper explaining the policies and procedures for conducting a pathology test. For the knowledge quiz, create a rough draft of the quiz questions. For the simulation, create a storyboard for the interactive scenario. For the form, create a pedagogical wrapper for using the assessment form. Create a pedagogical wrapper for the entire integrated learning experience. Then fashion a mockup of the learning experience structure within the learner interface (course website).

Obtain Feedback From Prospective Learners
Review your prototype with the learners you interviewed. You may also consider reaching out to friends and colleagues to review your prototype. Use the factors that influence the learner experience design when getting feedback related to the overall learning experience in Table 8.1. Figure 8.2 provides tips for obtaining learner feedback.

TABLE 8.1
Factors Influencing the Learning Experience Design

Factor	Description	Example
Useful	Ease of access and/or use.	Is the content useful? Does the content flow well? • Easy for the learners to become familiar with and competent • Easy for the learners to achieve their objective • Easy to recall the design aspect and how to use it on subsequent uses
Usable	Ease of access and/or use. It looks at three components: look, feel, and usability.	Is the content easily understandable? • Easy for the learners to become familiar with and competent on the first contact with the prototype design • Easy for the learners to achieve their objective through using the design aspect • Easy to recall the design aspect and how to use it subsequently if learners must reuse it It is important to analyze the learners' performance and concerns.

TABLE 8.1 (*Continued*)

Factor	Description	Example
Findable	Ability to easily find the material within the course website.	Can the learner effectively and efficiently locate the material?
Credible	Trust engendered in learners plays a part in the learning experience.	Security (i.e., terms of privacy) and easily accessible course features and policies can help create a sense of credibility for the learner.
Desirable	When the learner can form an emotional bond with the course, people, or learning environment. That means moving beyond usable and useful and on to developing something that creates that bond.	Does prototype design convey an emotional connection with the learner?
Accessible	Providing access to the prototype design by learners with a full range of abilities, including those with disabilities, such as having hearing, visual, or learning impairments.	Can the prototype design be accessed, understood, and used to the greatest extent possible by all people, regardless of their age, size, ability, or disability?
Valuable	Worth and relevance of the prototype design for the learners. The value of the prototype design might influence the learners to complete the online course.	Is the value of prototype design relevant to the learners' work or personal life?

Note. Adapted from Soegaard (2018).

Figure 8.2. Tips for obtaining learner feedback.

If seeking feedback in person:

- Provide any background information about the online course.
- Walk the reviewer through your prototype.
- Find out what resonates and what doesn't and why.
- Ask them to think out loud.
- Be sure to take notes.

If seeking feedback online:

- Provide any background information about the online course.
- Provide a set of questions you want the reviewer to answer.
- Find out what resonates and what doesn't and why.
- Ask the reviewer to record or write the prototype review.

Analyze the Feedback
Use the following questions to make decisions regarding refinements to the prototype design:

- Does the integrated learning experience meet the learner's needs?
- Does the integrated learning experience meet the course goals?
- Does the integrated learning experience meet the requirements in the problem statement?
- Does the material have coherence and flow?

Test

The testing phase involves trying out a more refined version of the prototype with learners at a small scale and getting feedback and advice. This phase can also be done in the form of walkthrough presentations with learners to get their reactions and suggestions. The testing shows where a prototype needs refinement and might even suggest looping back to the empathize mode to better understand learners and ideate a different alternative solution to the problem. Ask colleagues and learners to navigate the online environment from instructor and learner perspectives. In most cases, if adequate prototyping is done and enough feedback gathered to make refinements, the testing phase is a matter of tweaking and ironing out issues in the design of the learning activity and getting it ready to use in a real course context.

Testing is often done with a limited number of individuals to simulate the real-world context in which the actual learning occurs. In some cases,

TABLE 8.2
Test Survey

Criterion	Strongly Agree	Agree	Undecided	Disagree	Strongly Disagree
The learner interface is cohesive and intuitive.					
The lesson or unit structure is easily navigated.					
The learning activities and tasks infuse interest, curiosity, and challenge.					
Learning materials and tasks align with each other and create a cohesive learning experience.					
Learning materials within the lesson or unit communicate an emotional tone.					
The guided communication conveys an emotional connection.					
Learning tasks incorporate cognitive engagement.					
Assessment-based learning tasks infuse interest, challenge, and curiosity.					

Strengths of the Integrated Learning Experience

Suggestions for Improvement

during this phase the course designer might realize that in one of the former phases such as understanding the learners or defining the problem, the goal may need to be refined. The design process is iterative and may need to loop back to previous phases to refine ideas. Table 8.2 provides a sample test survey. The following criteria are useful for selecting and testing ideas:

- What works best and is most appealing for learners?
- What is feasible given existing resources?
- What best produces the desired learning outcomes?

Implement

This phase brings design thinking to some type of closure. After testing and refinements have been made based on feedback, the learning materials are ready to be incorporated into the actual course. Some people say that design is never complete, but at this point only minor tweaks may need to be made and elements polished. Feedback should still be obtained from learners to check for reusability and scalability.

Design thinking may seem like a lengthy process, but it can be done rapidly and informally. The approach used should be adapted to the specific situation to make the most sense for a particular situation and needs. The key facets of the design thinking mindset are to put users first, ask the right questions, be committed to exploring, and use rapid prototyping to test ideas and get feedback. This process is carried out in a more flexible and nonlinear fashion. Sometimes more than one phase can be worked on concurrently. An existing version of a learning material can be used as an initial prototype to get learner feedback and identify problems.

Guiding Design Questions and Design Strategies for Each Design Aspect

In this book, we have included guiding design questions from chapters 3 to 7 along with design strategies that answered these questions at the end of the chapters. Table 8.3 provides a summary of the guiding design questions and strategies for each design aspect as a quick reference when using design thinking.

Moving Forward for Designing the Online Learning Experience

As digital learning environments continue to evolve and online education becomes the standard in higher education contexts, creating quality online

TABLE 8.3

Summary of Guiding Design Questions and Strategies for Each Design Aspect

Design Aspect	Guiding Design Questions	Design Strategies
Course Structure and Learner Interface	• How can we use a course conceptual model to shape and focus the design of the course structure to better accomplish learning goals and meet learner needs?	• For knowledge-based courses, the structure should be organized around topic-based thematic units • For skill-based courses, the structure should be organized around constituent tasks
	• How can we design a course structure that is meaningful to learners and organized to better support specific kinds of learning outcomes?	• Align core topics or tasks with course goals • Get feedback and refine thematic units and explore strategies that support suitable instructional methods • Avoid fragmentation by creating cohesiveness and interrelationships of thematic units
	• How can we apply design thinking and UXD to create a learner-centered online course interface?	• Design a simple, usable, and appealing learner interface by obtaining learner feedback through iterative prototype testing
Content Interactions	• How can we start designing online content for different course design situations?	• For existing online courses, focus on making minor enhancements to information design, designing new learning activities, and incorporating external content • For converting classroom-based courses, rethink existing course model and structure, redesign and repurpose existing content, and incorporate external resources

(Continues)

TABLE 8.3 (*Continued*)

Design Aspect	Guiding Design Questions	Design Strategies
		• For creating new courses from scratch, do everything noted previously, and use design thinking to explore new technologies and digital pedagogies to enhance learning
	• How can we shift our thinking and practice to create pedagogically engaging content using new digital tools?	• Shift from fragmentation to integration of learner–content interactions • Shift from broad-brush to finely targeted content • Shift from decontextualized to contextualized content • Shift from single media to hybridized media content • Shift from cognitive dominance to emotional and behavioral interplay
	• How can we incorporate learning experience design strategies to create impactful learner–content interactions?	• Use pedagogical wrappers to integrate content. • Integrate rich content interactions through hybrid multimedia and instructional methods • Increase cognitive engagement and motivation through emotional design • Add context to content through stories and scenarios
Learning Activities	• How can we apply design thinking to create learning activities?	• Apply design thinking with an empathic mindset for the learner
	• How can we design engaging online learning activities?	• Use new technology tools and their affordances to create integrated and impactful learning activities

TABLE 8.3 (*Continued*)

Design Aspect	Guiding Design Questions	Design Strategies
	• How can we integrate learning activities into a course unit to support higher-order learning?	• Integrate multiple learning tasks into an inclusive learning activity
	• How can we design learning activities that help learners engage in deep learning?	• Use pedagogical wrappers to prepare learners cognitively and emotionally for the learning activity
Social Interactions	• How can a positive climate be set through social interactions?	• Set the stage for a positive climate through personal and professional stories, shared learning responsibility, pedagogical wrappers, and instructor involvement
	• How can social interactions create emotional connections?	• Create emotional connections through an intuitive learner interface, facilitated/guided and logistical/organizational communication
	• How can personalized communication be conveyed through social interactions?	• Use personalized communication for identifying participants through photos and graphics, sharing beliefs and values, and identifying people by name
	• How can learners be engaged in deep learning through social interactions?	• Promote deep learning through social engagement, scaffolding of social interactions, and course guidelines
	• How can learner involvement through social interactions enhance the flow of the course?	• Build learner involvement into the flow of the course through free-flow discussions, virtual office hours with a purpose, and end-of-course debriefings

(*Continues*)

TABLE 8.3 (*Continued*)

Design Aspect	Guiding Design Questions	Design Strategies
Assessments and Feedback	• How can we better design assessments and feedback considering stages of learner development and prior learning?	• Design assessments and feedback based on a learner growth mindset
	• How can we incorporate assessments throughout the online learning experience?	• Incorporate emotional and cognitive elements into assessments and feedback to infuse interest, challenge, and curiosity
	• How can we design assessment activities to be more engaging and conducive to deep learning experiences?	• Embed assessments and feedback into the learning experience to promote engagement and deep learning
	• How can we use assessments and feedback to establish and sustain learners' attention and motivation?	• Involve learners in assessments and feedback to spark interest and sustain motivation
	• How can we design assessments that help learners monitor their own learning?	• Include iterative self-assessment approaches to encourage self-regulated learning

courses now requires an integrative approach and a way of thinking that incorporates elements of user-centric interface design, emotional design, instructional message design, learner-centered design, and learner experience design. This approach involves the integration of the learner experience and online learning design, bringing distinctive ideas to produce creative solutions. This calls for a new set of learning design skills for instructors and course designers based on the concepts from these different fields of research and practice. By developing these skills, instructors and course designers can intentionally create personalized, engaging, and meaningful learning experiences for online learners.

Drawing from research in a variety of fields, we developed the integrated framework for designing the online learning experience as a way of thinking holistically about the learner through the four dimensions of learning and the five aspects of design. The framework is flexible and can help instructors and course designers set a frame of mind to build new courses, convert face-to-face courses to the online environment, or fine-tune existing online courses. We have also adapted design thinking concepts in the context of online learning as a mindset and a toolkit for creating learning experiences.

Our goal with this book is to provide a new approach for looking at the online learning experience and learner-centered design, with a focus on the cognitive, emotional, behavioral, and social needs of the learner considering the affordances of technologies. Our intent is not to provide a new model or recipe for designing online courses but rather to encourage others to think differently about learners, learning, and online course design. The core concepts, learning experience design principles, and integrated framework addressed in this book can serve as the language practitioners and scholars use to talk about learning experience design. The book is an attempt to help the emerging field develop more conceptual rigor. We hope to inspire instructors and course designers to consider these new skills and practices as they move forward into the future of online education.

Active learning strategies: A broad range of instructional approaches aimed at engaging learners as active participants in the learning process, bringing together knowing, doing, and active engagement in learning tasks involving multiple learner dimensions (cognitive, behavioral, and social)

Aesthetics: The look, feel, and visual attractiveness of the online course environment, particularly elements of the learner interface and content displays

Age differences (learner characteristics): Cognitive, emotional, behavioral, and social characteristics of learners within different age groupings

Aptitude (learner characteristics): Natural inborn talent or ability enabling an individual to perform certain types of work or tasks easily and quickly

Assessments and feedback (design aspect): Assessments as formative, occurring throughout the online course, and providing a detailed representation of a learner's progress and achievement; feedback as any messages from an instructor, formal or informal, in response to a learner action

Behavioral design principle: Focus on bridging the cognitive, emotional, and social dimensions of learning with opportunities for learners to apply and practice what they have learned

Behavioral dimension: One of the four dimensions of learning that focuses on observable learner actions or what they "do" in the online environment

Cognitive design principle: Focus on crafting learning interactions in ways that help learners use their cognitive capacities efficiently and effectively to accomplish learning goals

Cognitive dimension: One of the four dimensions of learning related to mental activities and processes that include perception, memory, classification, reasoning, critical thinking, and problem-solving

Concept map: Conceptual diagram that depicts relationships between concepts

Conceptual model: An image in the mind of a designer, prior to course development, that describes the purpose, function, look, and feel of an online course, which then shapes the course structure, user interface, and other features of the online course environment

Content interactions (design aspect): Creating, organizing, structuring, and presenting content to learners both synchronously and asynchronously using various media and message design strategies

Copresence: The sense of being together with other people in a shared online environment

Course design aspects: The five major course design focal points of the integrated framework for designing the online experience comprise the course structure and interface, content interactions, learning activities, social interactions, and assessments and feedback

Course structure and interface (design aspect): The first of five aspects of the integrated framework for designing the online learning experience that learners encounter as they use and navigate the online course space, the medium through which a learner's interaction with course content, the instructor, and other learners takes place

Culture and ethnicity (learner characteristics): Individual difference related to cultural dispositions and norms associated with learner ethnicity groups that can influence a learner's overall experience in online contexts

Deep learning: Learners' full engagement of mental resources to comprehend complicated material, understand complex concepts, solve problems requiring analysis and synthesis, and make difficult decisions by drawing upon discipline-specific knowledge and experience

Design thinking: Variously defined as a mindset, a problem-solving process, set of principles, and a toolkit for developing innovative learning solutions, products, and services

Didactic strategies: A teacher-centered method of instruction whereby an instructor communicates information to learners in a direct way such as through presentations and readings

Dimensions of learning: Four core human elements that when holistically integrated into the learning design process bring about meaningful and impactful learning experiences—the cognitive, emotional, behavioral, and social dimensions of learning

Emotional design: A term coined by cognitive psychologist Donald Norman based on the fact that behaviors, thinking, and emotions are intertwined; the idea that learning environments designed to be aesthetically pleasing and functional set the stage for positive learning experiences

Emotional design principle: Focus on design efforts to activate and sustain learner interest and motivation to more fully engage with every aspect of the online course experience

Emotional dimension: One of the four dimensions of learning, closely associated with learner motivation and encompassing both positive and negative emotions

Emotional presence: "The outward expression of emotion, affect, and feeling by individuals and among individuals in a community of inquiry, as they relate to and interact with the learning technology, course content, students, and the instructor" (Cleveland-Innes & Campbell, 2012, p. 283)

Empathic design: A learning design strategy and mindset that approaches learning design decisions from the learners' perspective, considering how they engage and interact with every other aspect of the learning environment

Explanatory presentations: A frequently used strategy of instruction wherein a subject matter expert or instructor attempts to provide answers to presumed learners' questions, clarify difficult concepts, and help learners in their understanding of a particular knowledge domain, mainly involving a didactic teaching strategy

Flow: A holistic sensation of total involvement, a state when a person performing an activity is totally engaged in the activity

Formative assessment: A method to improve learning and provide information about learner development during the online course

Four Cs of learner empathy: Caring about the learner's experience enough to invest effort in making it better; curiosity that provokes interest in what learners are thinking, feeling, behaving, and saying about their experience; conversations with learners about their course experiences, probing and listening to their ideas and suggestions; and changing or correcting the deficiencies in the course design aspects based on learner input

Gamification: "Using game-based mechanics, aesthetics, and game-thinking to engage people, motivate action, promote learning, and solve problems" (Kapp et al., 2014, p. 54)

Gender differences (learner characteristics): A mosaic of attributes that are shared by both males and females in diverse proportions with unlimited variation at the individual level

Growth mindset: Having an open mind or a positive outlook, embracing the idea that a person's capabilities and capacity to learn can be nurtured and developed through practice and hard work as opposed to inborn fixed abilities

Inductive strategies: Means by which learners acquire (induce) knowledge from concrete experiences or through challenging problems presented in the course, including problem-based and project-based learning activities

Information architecture: Part of learner interface design involving grouping, organizing, prioritizing, and presenting categories of content to give a sense of the scope and sequence of the course content, underlying menu design for course units, lessons, and topics as well as site navigation

Information design: Part of learner interface design focused on effective communication and presentation of content so that the learner can understand it more easily and use it to perform tasks

Integrated framework for designing the online learning experience: A mental model providing instructors and course designers with a practical, holistic, and evidence-based framework for achieving learner-centered design goals, resulting in the design of deeper, more meaningful and engaging learning experiences for online learners

Learner characteristics: Evidence-based categories of individual differences that influence the quality of learner interactions and learning outcomes in the online course environment, including prior knowledge, motivation, self-regulation, self-directedness, self-efficacy, perception of self-knowledge, personality traits, age differences, culture and ethnicity, aptitude, and gender differences

Learner interaction with technology: Clicking objects on the screen, scrolling, eye focusing, and other tasks performed related to accessing and interacting with content

Learner interface: The technology-based medium that a learner uses to facilitate all interactions in the online course space

Learner-centered design: A mindset and learning design strategy that approaches the design of each aspect of the online course environment from the perspective of a learner, applying the four dimensions of learning as a lens for envisioning learner interactions comprising the learning experience

Learning activities (design aspect): A skillfully designed form of learner interaction aimed at accomplishing higher-order learning objectives through tasks that actively engage learners at the cognitive, emotional, behavioral, and social dimensions of learning

Learning experience design: A process that involves creating technology-mediated interactions applied at the course, lesson, or activity levels in the online environment, holistic in that it integrates the cognitive, emotional, behavioral, and social dimensions of learning to promote learner engagement and deep learning

Learning experience design principles: A set of heuristics that guide design decisions for each of the five design aspects in the integrated framework for designing the online learning experience

Learning task: Performance-focused actions by learners that support the accomplishment of learning objectives, which at a course structural level, can be viewed as performance components of a larger skill or job, but at a modular level, as smaller action components of a learning activity

Look and feel: Part of the learner interface design of the online learning space related to the graphical surface layer of what the learner actually sees, hears, and interacts with on the screen

Motivation (learner characteristics): An internal force within individuals related to the emotional dimension that activates, directs, and sustains an individual's attention and behaviors toward achieving certain goals, measured in terms of invested mental effort

Participatory design: A design practice that directly involves input from multiple stakeholders such as learners, instructors, and course designers in making decisions regarding the design of the various aspects of the online learning environment

Pedagogical wrappers: An integration strategy using concise descriptors presented before a learner engages in a learning activity, content interaction, or structured social discourse, serving to make explicit the pedagogical purpose of the interaction and its connection with other course material and learning objectives

Perception of self-knowledge (learner characteristics): Learners' ability to accurately self-judge or assess their own learning, which in many cases tends to be self-inflated

Personality traits (learner characteristics): Individual differences in long-standing patterns in the way a person thinks, feels, and behaves

Personalized communication: A style of verbal and text-based communication that uses a conversational tone, often incorporating more personal pronouns, to create a deeper emotional connection with learners, shown to positively influence learner behavior, motivation, and engagement in online learning

Prior knowledge (learner characteristics): An individual's stored knowledge from previous learning experiences, often represented cognitively as schemas and neurologically as existing neural networks

Problem-based learning: An inductive and learner-centered strategy whereby learning occurs through the experience of solving open-ended problems that often involve all four dimensions of learning

Scenario-based activities: Inductive-type learning activities that use contextualization strategies to reinforce application of course content by incorporating story-like narratives of authentic situations likely to be encountered in the real world, with well-designed scenario-based activities integrating all four learning dimensions

Self-directedness (learner characteristics): Learners' ability to guide and direct their own learning with moral, emotional, and intellectual autonomy

Self-efficacy (learner characteristics): A learner trait involving self-perceptions and beliefs about personal ability to understand certain content material and perform learning tasks, with perceived self-efficacy able to influence an individual's effort and persistence in challenging learning situations and impact learning outcomes in both positive and negative ways

Self-regulation (learner characteristics): The degree to which students are "metacognitively, motivationally, and behaviorally active participants in their own learning process" (Zimmerman & Martinez-Pons, 1988, p. 284)

Seven Cs framework: A set of design principles for crafting pedagogically compelling and interactive story narratives for scenario-based learning activities, with well-designed scenarios integrating seven elements into a story narrative: challenge, context, characters, content, choices, consequences, and connections

Shallow learning: Also referred to as *surface learning*, emphasizes memorization of new ideas, facts, and information which tends to result in minimal depth of conceptual understanding and cognitive processing

Social design principle: Focus on social interactions involving discourse between instructor and learner and among learners

Social dimension: One or the four learning dimensions, focused on the relationship of individuals in a learning environment, defined as having "a sense of being with others and responding to each other" (Lehman & Conceição, 2010, p. 16)

Social interactions (design aspect): One of the five aspects of the integrated framework for designing the online learning experience, focused on the design of technology-mediated interpersonal communications between individuals, groups, and instructor to facilitate learning

Spacing and interleaving assessments: Alternating assessments between content presentations and learning activities or embedding assessments and connecting them to new learning to create relevant associations of content

Story-based online content: A contextualization strategy whereby relevant stories associated with learning objectives and course subject matter are integrated into instructional units, lessons, and learning activities to reinforce application of important concepts and principles and to make connections to real-world experiences

Summative assessment: Conducted at the end of the course, determination whether learners met the course outcomes

User experience design: Any design interaction with any product, artifact, or system focusing on people's needs, reactions, and behaviors, taking "the user into account every step of the way" (Garrett, 2011, p. 17)

REFERENCES

Adams, T., & Evans, R. S. (2004). Educating the educators: Outreach to the college of education distance faculty and Native American students. *Journal of Library Administration, 41*(1/2), 3–18. https://doi.org/10.1300/J111v41n01_02

Allen, M. W. (2011). *Designing successful e-learning: Forget what you know about instructional design and do something interesting* (Vol. 2). Wiley.

Allen, M. (2012). *Leaving ADDIE for SAM: An agile model for developing the best learning experiences*. American Society for Training and Development.

Anderson, L. W., & Krathwohl, D. R. (2001). *A taxonomy for learning, teaching, and assessing: A revision of Bloom's taxonomy of educational objectives*. Longman.

Aragon, S. R. (2003). Creating social presence in online environments. *New Directions for Adult and Continuing Education, 100*, 57–68. https://doi.org/10.1002/ace.119

Baker, C. (2010). The impact of instructor immediacy and presence for online student affective learning, cognition, and motivation. *Journal of Educators Online, 7*(1). https://files.eric.ed.gov/fulltext/EJ904072.pdf

Bandura, A. (1997). *Self-efficacy: The exercise of control*. W H Freeman/Times Books/Henry Holt & Co.

Bennett, S., Agostinho, S., & Lockyer, L. (2017). The process of designing for learning: Understanding university teachers' design work. *Educational Technology Research and Development, 65*(1), 125–145. https://doi.org/10.1007/s11423-016-9469-y

Bierton, S., Wilson, E., Kistler, M., Flowers, J., & Jones, D. (2016). A comparison of higher order thinking skills demonstrated in synchronous and asynchronous online college discussion posts. *NACTA Journal, 60*(1), 14–21. https://www.nactateachers.org/attachments/article/2377/7%20%20Brierton_NACTA%20Journal.pdf

Biesenbach-Lucas, S. (2003). Asynchronous discussion groups in teacher training classes: Perceptions of native and non-native students. *Journal of Asynchronous Learning Networks, 7*(3), 24–46. http://doi.org/10.24059/olj.v7i3.1843

Bloom, B., & Krathwohl, D. R. (1956). *Taxonomy of educational objectives: The classification of educational goals, by a committee of college and university examiners—Handbook 1: Cognitive domain*. Longman.

Bolkan, S., Goodboy, A. K., & Kelsey, D. M. (2016). Instructor clarity and student motivation: Academic performance as a product of students' ability and motivation to process instructional material. *Communication Education, 65*(2), 129–148. https://doi.org/10.1080/03634523.2015.1079329

Bowen, J. A. (2012). *Teaching naked: How moving technology out of your college classroom will improve student learning.* Jossey-Bass.

Boyer, N. R., Maher, P. A., & Kirkman, S. (2006). Transformative learning in online settings: The use of self-direction, metacognition, and collaborative learning. *Journal of Transformative Education, 4*(4), 335–361. https://doi .org/10.1177/1541344606295318

Branch, R. M. (2009). *Instructional design: The ADDIE approach.* Springer.

Brenner, W., Uebernickel, F., & Abrell, T. (2016). Design thinking as mindset, process, and toolbox. In W. Brenner & F. Uebernickel (Eds.), *Design thinking for innovation* (pp. 3–21). Springer.

Britt, M. A., & Sommer, J. (2004). Facilitating textual integration with macrostructure focusing tasks. *Reading Psychology, 25*(4), 313–339. https://doi .org/10.1080/02702710490522658

Broadbent, J., & Poon, W. L. (2015). Self-regulated learning strategies and academic achievement in online higher education learning environments: A systematic review. *The Internet and Higher Education, 27,* 1–13. https://doi.org/10.1016/ j.iheduc.2015.04.007

Brockett, R. G., & Hiemstra, R. (1991). *Self-direction in adult learning: Perspectives on theory, research, and practice.* Routledge.

Brown, M., Dehoney, J., & Millichap, N. (2015, April). The next generation digital learning environment: A report on research. *Educause.* https://library.educause .edu/-/media/files/library/2015/4/eli3035-pdf.pdf

Brucker, B., Scheiter, K., & Gerjets, P. (2014). Learning with dynamic and static visualizations: Realistic details only benefit learners with high visuospatial abilities. *Computers in Human Behavior, 36,* 330–339. https://doi.org/10.1016/ j.chb.2014.03.077

Bullen, M., Morgan, T., & Qayyum, A. (2011). Digital learners in higher education: Generation is not the issue. *Canadian Journal of Learning and Technology/La revue Canadienne de l'apprentissage et de la Technologie, 37*(1), 1–24. https://doi .org/10.21432/T2NC7B

Bundy, C., & Howles, L. (2017, October 23). Interactive case scenarios: The 7Cs framework. *Educause.* https://library.educause.edu/resources/2017/10/interactive -case-scenarios-the-7cs-framework

Busselle, R., & Bilandzic, H. (2008). Fictionality and perceived realism in experiencing stories: A model of narrative comprehension and engagement. *Communication Theory, 18*(2), 255–280. https://doi.org/10.1111/j.1468-2885.2008 .00322.x

Calvo, R. A., & D'Mello, S. K. (Eds.). (2011). *New perspectives on affect and learning technologies* (Vol. 3). Springer.

Cañas, A. J., Reiska, P., & Möllits, A. (2017). Developing higher-order thinking skills with concept mapping: A case of pedagogic frailty. *Knowledge Management & e-Learning, 9*(3), 348–365. https://doi.org/10.34105/j.kmel.2017.09 .021

Candy, P. C. (1991). *Self-direction for lifelong learning. A comprehensive guide to theory and practice.* Jossey-Bass.

Cazan, A. M. (2013). Teaching self-regulated learning strategies for psychology students. *Procedia-Social and Behavioral Sciences, 78*, 743–747. https://doi.org/10.1016/j.sbspro.2013.04.387

Chang, C. S., Liu, E. Z. F., Sung, H. Y., Lin, C. H., Chen, N. S., & Cheng, S. S. (2014). Effects of online college student's Internet self-efficacy on learning motivation and performance. *Innovations in Education and Teaching International, 51*(4), 366–377. https://doi.org/10.1080/14703297.2013.771429

Chang, S. C., & Tung, F. C. (2008). An empirical investigation of students' behavioural intentions to use the online learning course websites. *British Journal of Educational Technology, 39*(1), 71–83. https://doi.org/10.1111/j.1467-8535.2007.00742.x

Cho, M. H., & Cho, Y. (2014). Instructor scaffolding for interaction and students' academic engagement in online learning: Mediating role of perceived online class goal structures. *The Internet and Higher Education, 21*, 25–30. https://doi.org/10.1016/j.iheduc.2013.10.008

Cho, V., Cheng, T. E., & Lai, W. J. (2009). The role of perceived user–interface design in continued usage intention of self-paced e-learning tools. *Computers & Education, 53*(2), 216–227. https://doi.org/10.1016/j.compedu.2009.01.014

Clark, R. (2013). Why games don't teach. *Learning Solutions Magazine.* https://learningsolutionsmag.com/articles/1106/why-games-dont-teach

Clark, R. C. (2013). *Scenario-based e-learning: Evidence-based guidelines for online workforce learning.* Wiley.

Clark, R. C., & Mayer, R. E. (2016). *E-learning and the science of instruction: Proven guidelines for consumers and designers of multimedia learning.* Wiley.

Clark, R. C., Nguyen, F., & Sweller, J. (2011). *Efficiency in learning: Evidence-based guidelines to manage cognitive load.* Wiley.

Clark, R. C., Nguyen, F., Sweller, J., & Baddeley, M. (2006). *Efficiency in learning: Evidence-based guidelines to manage cognitive load.* Wiley.

Clark, R. E., & Feldon, D. F. (2014). Ten common but questionable principles of multimedia learning. In R. E. Mayer (Ed.), *The Cambridge handbook of multimedia learning* (pp. 151–173). Cambridge University Press.

Cleveland-Innes, M., & Campbell, P. (2012). Emotional presence, learning, and the online learning environment. *The International Review of Research in Open and Distributed Learning, 13*(4), 269–292. https://doi.org/10.19173/irrodl.v13i4.1234

Coates, H., James, R., & Baldwin, G. (2005). A critical examination of the effects of learning management systems on university teaching and learning. *Tertiary Education and Management, 11*, 19–36. https://doi.org/10.1007/s11233-004-3567-9

Cohen, A., & Baruth, O. (2017). Personality, learning, and satisfaction in fully online academic courses. *Computers in Human Behavior, 72*, 1–12. https://doi.org/10.1016/j.chb.2017.02.030

Conceição, S. C., & Lehman, R. M. (2011). *Managing online instructor workload: Strategies for finding balance and success.* Jossey-Bass.

Conceição, S. C. O., Baldor, M. J., & Desnoyers, C. A. (2009). Facilitating individual construction of knowledge in an online community of learning and inquiry through concept maps. In R. Marriott & P. Torres (Eds.), *Handbook of research on collaborative learning using concept mapping* (pp. 100–119). IGI Global.

Conceição, S. C. O., & Schmidt, S. (2010). How non-content-related forums influence social presence in the online learning environment. *Indian Journal of Open Learning, 19*(2), 73–85.

Costa, P. T., & McCrae, R. (1992). *The NEO Personality Inventory–Revised (NEO PI-R)*. Psychological Assessment Resources.

Crawford, J. D., & Stankov, L. (1996). Age differences in the realism of confidence judgements: A calibration study using tests of fluid and crystallized intelligence. *Learning and Individual Differences, 8*(2), 83–103. https://doi.org/10.1016/S1041-6080(96)90027-8

Crisp, G. T. (2012). Integrative assessment: Reframing assessment practice for current and future learning. *Assessment & Evaluation in Higher Education, 37*(1), 33–43. https://doi.org/10.1080/02602938.2010.494234

Croxton, R. A. (2014). The role of interactivity in student satisfaction and persistence in online learning. *Journal of Online Learning and Teaching, 10*(2), 314.

Crozier, W. R. (1997). *Individual learners: Personality differences in education*. Routledge.

Dabbagh, N. (2007). The online learner: Characteristics and pedagogical implications. *Contemporary Issues in Technology and Teacher Education, 7*(3), 217–226.

Dennen, V. P., Aubteen Darabi, A., & Smith, L. J. (2007). Instructor–learner interaction in online courses: The relative perceived importance of particular instructor actions on performance and satisfaction. *Distance Education, 28*(1), 65–79. https://doi.org/10.1080/01587910701305319

DiSalvo, B., Yip, J., Bonsignore, E., & DiSalvo, C. (Eds.). (2017). *Participatory design for learning: Perspectives from practice and research*. Taylor & Francis.

D'Mello, S., Lehman, B., Pekrun, R., & Graesser, A. (2014). Confusion can be beneficial for learning. *Learning and Instruction, 29*, 153–170. https://doi.org/10.1016/j.learninstruc.2012.05.003

Dunlosky, J., Hertzog, C., Kennedy, M. R., & Thiede, K. W. (2005). The self-monitoring approach for effective learning. *Cognitive Technology, 10*(1), 4–11.

Dunlosky, J., & Rawson, K. A. (2012). Overconfidence produces underachievement: Inaccurate self-evaluations undermine students' learning and retention. *Learning and Instruction, 22*(4), 271–280. https://doi.org/10.1016/j.learninstruc.2011.08.003

Dweck, C. S. (2006). *Mindset: The new psychology of success*. Ballantine Books.

Entwistle, N., & Waterson, S. (1988). Approaches to studying and levels of processing in university students. *Journal of Educational Psychology, 58*, 258–265. https://doi.org/10.1111/j.2044-8279.1988.tb00901.x

Feldon, D. F., Callan, G., Juth, S., & Jeong, S. (2019). Cognitive load as motivational cost. *Educational Psychology Review, 31*, 319–337. https://doi.org/10.1007/s10648-019-09464-6

Felten, P., & Finley, A. (2019). *Transparent design in higher education teaching and leadership: A guide to implementing the transparency framework institution-wide to improve learning and retention*. Stylus.

Fessenden, F. (2017). *First impressions matter: How designers can support humans' automatic cognitive processing.* Nielsen Norman Group. http://www.nngroup .com/articles/first-impressions-human-automaticity/

Fink, L. D. (2013). *Creating significant learning experiences: An integrated approach to designing college courses.* Wiley.

Fry, R. (2016). *Millennials overtake Baby Boomers as America's largest generation.* Pew Research Center. http://www.pewresearch.org/fact-tank/2016/04/25/millennials -overtake-baby-boomers/

Gagne, R. M., & Briggs, L. J. (1979). *Principles of instructional design.* Holt, Rine- hart & Winston.

Gallardo-Echenique, E. E., Marqués-Molías, L., Bullen, M., & Strijbos, J. W. (2015). Let's talk about digital learners in the digital era. *The International Review of Research in Open and Distributed Learning, 16*(3), 156–187. https://doi .org/10.19173/irrodl.v16i3.2196

Garrett, J. J. (2011). *The elements of user experience: User-centered design for the web and beyond.* New Riders.

Garrison, D. R. (1997). Self-directed learning: Toward a comprehensive model. *Adult Education Quarterly, 48*(1), 18–33. https://doi.org/10.1177/07417136970 4800103

Garrison, D. R., Anderson, T., & Archer, W. (2003). A theory of critical inquiry in online distance education. *Handbook of Distance Education, 1,* 113–127.

Giamellaro, M. (2017). Dewey's yardstick: Contextualization as a crosscutting measure of experience in education and learning. *Sage Open, 7*(1). https://doi .org/10.1177/2158244017700463

Grabinger, R. S., & Dunlap, J. C. (1995). Rich environments for active learning: A definition. *ALT-J, 3*(2), 5–34. https://doi.org/10.1080/0968776950030202

Graesser, A., & D'Mello, S. K. (2011). Theoretical perspectives on affect and deep learning. In R. A. Calvo & S. K. D'Mello (Eds.), *New perspectives on affect and learning technologies* (Vol. 3; pp. 11–21). Springer.

Graesser, A., Ozuru, Y., & Sullins, J. (2010). What is a good question? In M. G. McKeown & L. Kucan (Eds.), *Bringing reading research to life* (pp. 112–141). Guilford.

Harley, A. (2017). *Functional fixedness stops you from having innovative ideas.* Nielsen Norman Group. https://www.nngroup.com/articles/functional-fixedness/

Hassenzahl, M. (2004). The interplay of beauty, goodness, and usability in inter- active products. *Human-Computer Interaction, 19*(4), 319–349. https://doi .org/10.1207/s15327051hci1904_2

Hazrati-Viari, A., Rad, A. T., & Torabi, S. S. (2012). The effect of personality traits on academic performance: The mediating role of academic motivation. *Procedia-Social and Behavioral Sciences, 32,* 367–371. https://doi.org/10.1016/ j.sbspro.2012.01.055

Horn, R. E. (1989). Mapping hypertext: Analysis, linkage, and display of knowledge for the next generation of on-line text and graphics. Lexington Institute.

Horn, R. E. (1998a). Structured writing as a paradigm. In A. Romiszowski & C. Dills (Eds.), *Instructional development: State of the art* (pp. 697–714). Educational Technology Publications.

Horn, R. E. (1998b). *Visual language: Global communication for the 21st century.* XPlane.

Horn, R. E., Nicol, E. H., Kleinman, J. C., & Grace, M. G. (1969). *Information mapping for learning and reference.* Information Resources.

Horton, W. (2012). *E-learning by design.* Wiley.

Huchingson, R. D. (1981). *New horizons for human factors in design.* McGraw-Hill.

Huffman, A. H., Whetten, J., & Huffman, W. H. (2013). Using technology in higher education: The influence of gender roles on technology self-efficacy. *Computers in Human Behavior, 29*(4), 1779–1786. https://doi.org/10.1016/j.chb.2013.02.012

Ibarra, R. A. (2000). *Studying Latinos in a "virtual" university: Reframing diversity and academic culture change* (Occasional Paper No. 68). Julian Samora Research Institute, Michigan State University.

Interaction Design Foundation. (n.d.). *Conducting interviews with empathy.* https://public-media.interaction-design.org/pdf/Conducting-an-Interview-with-Empathy.pdf

Jackson, G. T., & Graesser, A. C. (2007). Content matters: An investigation of feedback categories within an ITS. *Frontiers in Artificial Intelligence and Applications, 158,* 127.

Jelfs, A., & Richardson, J. T. (2013). The use of digital technologies across the adult life span in distance education. *British Journal of Educational Technology, 44*(2), 338–351. https://doi.org/10.1111/j.1467-8535.2012.01308.x

Jeong, A., & Davidson-Shivers, G. V. (2006). The effects of gender interaction patterns on student participation in computer-supported collaborative argumentation. *Educational Technology Research and Development, 54*(6), 543–568. https://doi.org/10.1007/s11423-006-0636-4

Jonassen, D. H. (Ed.). (2014). Assessing problem solving. In *Handbook of research on educational communications and technology* (pp. 819–828). Springer.

Jonassen, D. H., Beissner, K., & Yacci, M. (1993). *Structural knowledge: Techniques for representing, conveying, and acquiring structural knowledge.* Routledge.

Jonassen, D. H., Reeves, T. C., Hong, N., Harvey, D., & Peters, K. (1997). Concept mapping as cognitive learning and assessment tools. *Journal of Interactive Learning Research, 8*(3), 289.

Joo, Y. J., Lim, K. Y., & Kim, E. K. (2011). Online university students' satisfaction and persistence: Examining perceived level of presence, usefulness and ease of use as predictors in a structural model. *Computers & Education, 57*(2), 1654–1664. https://doi.org/10.1016/j.compedu.2011.02.008

Kahneman, D. (2015). *Thinking, fast and slow.* Farrar, Straus, and Giroux.

Kapp, K., Blair, L., & Mesch, R. (2014). *The gamification of learning and instruction fieldbook.* Wiley.

Ke, F. (2010). Examining online teaching, cognitive, and social presence for adult students. *Computers & Education, 55*(2), 808–820. https://doi.org/10.1016/j.compedu.2010.03.013

Ke, F., & Kwak, D. (2013). Online learning across ethnicity and age: A study on learning interaction participation, perception, and learning satisfaction. *Computers & Education, 61,* 43–51. https://doi.org/10.1016/j.compedu.2012.09.003

Kellen, V. (2017, July/August). The origins of innovation in the EdTech ecosystem. *Educause Review, 52*(4), 50–56. https://er.educause.edu/articles/2017/7/the-origins-of-innovation-in-the-edtech-ecosystem

Keller, J., & Burkman, E. (1993). Motivation principles. In M. L. Fleming & W. H. Levie (Eds.), *Instructional message design: Principles from the behavioral and cognitive sciences* (pp. 3–49). Educational Technology Publications.

Keller, J. M. (1999). Using the ARCS motivational process in computer-based instruction and distance education. *New Directions for Teaching and Learning, 78,* 37–47. https://doi.org/10.1002/tl.7804

Kidd, C., & Hayden, B. Y. (2015). The psychology and neuroscience of curiosity. *Neuron, 88*(3), 449–460. https://doi.org/10.1016/j.neuron.2015.09.010

Klassen, R. M., Krawchuk, L. L., & Rajani, S. (2008). Academic procrastination of undergraduates: Low self-efficacy to self-regulate predicts higher levels of procrastination. *Contemporary Educational Psychology, 33*(4), 915–931. https://doi.org/10.1016/j.cedpsych.2007.07.001

Koh, J. H. L., Chai, C. S., Wong, B., & Hong, H. Y. (2015). *Design thinking for education: Conceptions and applications in teaching and learning.* Springer.

Kolb, A. Y., & Kolb, D. A. (2009). Experiential learning theory: A dynamic, holistic approach to management learning, education and development. In S. Armstrong & C. V. Fukami (Eds.), *The SAGE handbook of management learning, education and development* (pp. 42–68). Sage.

Könings, K. D., Seidel, T., & van Merriënboer, J. G. (2014). Participatory design of learning environments: Integrating perspectives of students, teachers, and designers. *Instructional Science, 42*(1), 1–9. https://doi.org/10.1007/s11251-013-9305-2

Koriat, A., & Bjork, R. A. (2005). Illusions of competence in monitoring one's knowledge during study. *Journal of Experimental Psychology: Learning, Memory, and Cognition, 31*(2), 187. https://doi.org/10.1037/0278-7393.31.2.187

Kreber, C. (2004). An analysis of two models of reflection and their implications for educational development. *International Journal for Academic Development, 9*(1), 29–49. https://doi.org/10.1080/1360144042000296044

Kruger, J., & Dunning, D. (1999). Unskilled and unaware of it: How difficulties in recognizing one's own incompetence lead to inflated self-assessments. *Journal of Personality and Social Psychology, 77*(6), 1121–1134. https://doi.org/10.1037/0022-3514.77.6.1121

Kurt, S. (2017). ADDIE model: Instructional design. *Educational Technology.* https://educationaltechnology.net/the-addie-model-instructional-design/

Ladyshewsky, R. (2013). Instructor presence in online courses and student satisfaction. *International Journal for the Scholarship of Teaching and Learning, 7*(1), 1–23.

Lai, K. W., & Hong, K. S. (2015). Technology use and learning characteristics of students in higher education: Do generational differences exist? *British Journal of Educational Technology, 46*(4), 725–738. https://doi.org/10.1111/bjet.12161

Lavie, T., & Tractinsky, N. (2004). Assessing dimensions of perceived visual aesthetics of web sites. *International Journal of Human-Computer Studies, 60*(3), 269–298. https://doi.org/10.1016/j.ijhcs.2003.09.002

Learner-Centered Principles Work Group of the American Psychological Association's Board of Educational Affairs. (1997). *Learner-centered psychological principles: A framework for school reform and redesign.* American Psychological Association.

Lee, J. (2014). An exploratory study of effective online learning: Assessing satisfaction levels of graduate students of mathematics education associated with human and design factors of an online course. *The International Review of Research in Open and Distributed Learning, 15*(1), 111–132. https://doi.org/10.19173/irrodl.v15i1.1638

Lehman, R. M., & Conceição, S. C. (2010). *Creating a sense of presence in online teaching: How to "be there" for distance learners.* Jossey-Bass.

Lehman, R. M., & Conceição, S. C. O. (2014). *Motivating and retaining online students: Research-based strategies that work.* Jossey-Bass.

Lindgaard, G., Fernandes, G., Dudek, C., & Brown, J. (2006). Attention web designers: You have 50 milliseconds to make a good first impression! *Behaviour and Information Technology, 25*(2), 115–126. https://doi.org/10.1080/01449290500330448

Loderer, K., Pekrun, R., & Lester, J. C. (2018). Beyond cold technology: A systematic review and meta-analysis on emotions in technology-based learning environments. *Learning and Instruction.* https://doi.org/10.1016/j.learninstruc.2018.08.002

Lohr, L. L. (2000). Designing the instructional interface. *Computers in Human Behavior, 16*(2), 161–182. https://doi.org/10.1016/S0747-5632(99)00057-6

Marks, R. B., Sibley, S. D., & Arbaugh, J. B. (2005). A structural equation model of predictors for effective online learning. *Journal of Management Education, 29*(4), 531–563. https://doi.org/10.1177/1052562904271199

Mason, B. J., & Bruning, R. H. (2001). *Providing feedback in computer-based instruction: What the research tells us* (CLASS Research Report No. 9). Center for Instructional Innovation, University of Nebraska-Lincoln. https://www.researchgate.net/publication/247291218_Providing_Feedback_in_Computer-based_Instruction_What_the_Research_Tells_Us

Mayer, R., Fennell, S., Farmer, L., & Campbell, J. (2004). A personalization effect in multimedia learning: Students learn better when words are in conversational style rather than formal style. *Journal of Education Psychology, 96*(2), 389–395. https://doi.org/10.1037/0022-0663.96.2.389

Mayer, R. E. (2014). Multimedia instruction. In J. M. Spector, M. D. Merrill, J. Elen, & M. J. Bishop (Eds.), *Handbook of research on educational communications and technology* (pp. 385–399). Springer.

Mayer, R. E., Griffith, E., Jurkowitz, I. T., & Rothman, D. (2008). Increased inter-estingness of extraneous details in a multimedia science presentation leads to decreased learning. *Journal of Experimental Psychology: Applied, 14*(4), 329–339. https://doi.org/10.1037/a0013835

Mayer, R. E., & Sims, V. K. (1994). For whom is a picture worth a thousand words? Extensions of a dual-coding theory of multimedia learning. *Journal of Educational Psychology, 86*(3), 389–401. https://doi.org/10.1037/0022-0663.86.3.389

Mazzolini, M., & Maddison, S. (2003). Sage, guide or ghost? The effect of instructor intervention on student participation in online discussion forums. *Computers and Education, 40*(3), 237–253. https://doi.org/10.1016/S0360-1315(02)00129-X

McCracken, J., Cho, S., Sharif, A., Wilson, B., & Miller, J. (2012). Principled assessment strategy design for online courses and programs. *Electronic Journal of E-learning, 10*(1), 107–119.

McEvoy, D., & Cowan, B. R. (2016). The importance of emotional design to create engaging digital HCI learning experiences. *On the Horizon, 9*(5), 1–6. http://doi.org/10.13140/RG.2.2.17162.26560

Medina, J. (2014). *Brain rules: 12 principles for surviving and thriving at work, home, and school.* Pear Press.

Merrills, J. M. S. (2010). *Factors affecting nontraditional African American students' participation in online world literature classes* [Doctoral dissertation, The University of North Carolina at Greensboro].

Meyer, K. (2017). *The aesthetic-usability effect.* Nielsen Norman Group. https://www.nngroup.com/articles/aesthetic-usability-effect/

Miller, M. D. (2014). *Minds online: Teaching effectively with technology.* Harvard University Press.

Molloy, E. K., & Boud, D. (2014). Feedback models for learning, teaching, and performance. In H. D. Jonassen (Ed.), *Handbook of research on educational communications and technology* (pp. 413–525). Springer.

Moore, M. G. (2013). The theory of transactional distance. In M. G. Moore (Ed.), *Handbook of distance education* (pp. 84–103). Routledge.

Ngeow, K., & Yoon-San, K. (2003). *Learning through discussion: Designing tasks for critical inquiry and reflective learning* (EDO-CS-03-06). The Clearinghouse on Reading, English and Communication, Indiana University School of Education.

Nielsen, J. (2017). *A 100-year view of user experience.* Nielsen Norman Group. https://www.nngroup.com/articles/100-years-ux/

Norman, D. (1990). Why interfaces don't work. In B. Laurel & S. J. Mountford (Eds.), *The art of human computer interface design* (pp. 209–219). Addison Wesley Longman.

Norman, D. (2016). The future of design: When you come to a fork in the road, take it. *She Ji: The Journal of Design Economics and Innovation, 2*(4), 343–348. https://doi.org/10.1016/j.sheji.2017.07.003

Norman, D. A. (2004). *Emotional design: Why we love (or hate) everyday things.* Basic Civitas Books.

Norman, D. A. (2005, July–August). Human-centered design considered harmful. *Interactions, 12*(4), 14–19. https://doi.org/10.1145/1070960.1070976

Oberauer, K., & Kliegl, R. (2001). Beyond resources: Formal models of complexity effects and age differences in working memory. *European Journal of Cognitive Psychology, 13*(1–2), 187–215. https://doi.org/10.1080/09541440042000278

O'Brien, H., & Lebow, M. (2013). Mixed-methods approach to measuring user experience in online news interactions. *Journal of the American Society for Information Science and Technology, 64*(8), 1543–1556. https://doi.org/10.1002/asi.22871

Offir, B., Lev, Y., & Bezalel, R. (2008). Surface and deep learning processes in distance education: Synchronous versus asynchronous systems. *Computers & Education, 51*(3), 1172–1183. https://doi.org/10.1016/j.compedu.2007.10.009

Orcutt, J. M., & Dringus, L. P. (2017). Beyond being there: Practices that establish presence, engage students and influence intellectual curiosity in a structured online learning environment. *Online Learning, 21*(3), 15–35. https://doi.org/10.24059/olj.v21i3.1231

Orlando, J. (2016). A comparison of text, voice, and screencasting feedback to online students. *American Journal of Distance Education, 30*(3), 156–166. https://doi.org/10.1080/08923647.2016.1187472

Oudeyer, P. Y., Gottlieb, J., & Lopes, M. (2016). Intrinsic motivation, curiosity, and learning: Theory and applications in educational technologies. *Progress in Brain Research, 229*, 257–284. https://doi.org/10.1016/bs.pbr.2016.05.005

Paas, F., Tuovinen, J. E., van Merriënboer, J. G., & Darabi, A. A. (2005). A motivational perspective on the relation between mental effort and performance: Optimizing learner involvement in instruction. *Educational Technology Research and Development, 53*(3), 25–34. https://doi.org/10.1007/BF02504795

Panadero, E., Jonsson, A., & Botella, J. (2017). Effects of self-assessment on self-regulated learning and self-efficacy: Four meta-analyses. *Educational Research Review, 22*, 74–98. https://doi.org/10.1016/j.edurev.2017.08.004

Park, J.-H., & Choi, H. J. (2009). Factors influencing adult learners' decision to drop out or persist in online learning. *Educational Technology & Society, 12*(4), 207–217.

Paulus, T. M., Horvitz, B., & Shi, M. (2006). "Isn't it just like our situation?" Engagement and learning in an online story-based environment. *Educational Technology Research and Development, 54*(4), 355–385. https://doi.org/10.1007/s11423-006-9604-2

Pearce, J. M., Ainley, M., & Howard, S. (2005). The ebb and flow of online learning. *Computers in Human Behavior, 21*(5), 745–771. https://doi.org/10.1016/j.chb.2004.02.019

Pekrun, R. (2011). Emotions as drivers of learning and cognitive development. In R. A. Calvo & S. K. D'Mello (Eds.), *New perspectives on affect and learning technologies* (pp. 23–39). Springer.

Pfeffer, J., & Sutton, R. I. (2000). *The knowing–doing gap: How smart companies turn knowledge into action.* Harvard Business.

Plass, J. L., & Kaplan, U. (2016). Emotional design in digital media for learning. In S. Tettegah & M. Gartmeier (Eds.), *Emotions, technology, design, and learning* (pp. 131–162). Elsevier.

Postareff, L., & Lindblom-Ylänne, S. (2008). Variation in teachers' descriptions of teaching: Broadening the understanding of teaching in higher education. *Learning and Instruction, 18*(2), 109–120. https://doi.org/10.1016/j.learninstruc.2007.01.008

Puzziferro, M. (2008). Online technologies self-efficacy and self-regulated learning as predictors of final grade and satisfaction in college-level online courses. *The American Journal of Distance Education, 22*(2), 72–89. https://doi.org/10.1080/08923640802039024

Reeve, J., & Tseng, C. M. (2011). Agency as a fourth aspect of students' engagement during learning activities. *Contemporary Educational Psychology, 36*(4), 257–267. https://doi.org/10.1016/j.cedpsych.2011.05.002

Reichelt, M., Kämmerer, F. Niegemann, H., & Zander, S. (2014). Talk to me personally: Personalization of language style in computer-based learning. *Computers in Human Behavior, 35,* 199–210. https://doi.org/10.1016/j.chb.2014.03.005

Roediger, H. L., III, Putnam, A. L., & Smith, M. A. (2011). Ten benefits of testing and their applications to educational practice. *Psychology of Learning and Motivation, 55,* 1–36. https://doi.org/10.1016/B978-0-12-387691-1.00001-6

Roediger, H. L., III, & Pyc, M. A. (2012). Inexpensive techniques to improve education: Applying cognitive psychology to enhance educational practice. *Journal of Applied Research in Memory and Cognition, 1*(4), 242–248. https://doi.org/10.1016/j.jarmac.2012.09.002

Rogerson-Revell, P. (2015). Constructively aligning technologies with learning and assessment in a distance education master's programme. *Distance Education, 36*(1), 129–147. https://doi.org/10.1080/01587919.2015.1019972

Romiszowski, A. J. (1981). *Designing instructional systems: Decision making in course planning and curriculum design.* Nichols Publishing.

Rosen, L. D. (2011). Teaching the iGeneration. *Teaching Screenagers, 68*(5), 10–15. http://www.ascd.org/publications/educational-leadership/feb11/vol68/num05/Teaching-the-iGeneration.aspx

Rosenberg, M. J., & Foreman, S. (2014). *Learning and performance ecosystems: Strategy, technology, impact, and challenges* (White paper). The eLearning Guild.

Rouet, J. F., & Britt, M. A. (2014). Multimedia learning from multiple documents. In R. E. Mayer (Ed.), *The Cambridge handbook of multimedia learning* (pp. 813–841). Cambridge University Press.

Russo, T. C., & Campbell, S. W. (2004). Perceptions of mediated presence in an asynchronous online course: Interplay of communication behaviors and medium. *Distance Education, 25*(2), 215–232. https://doi.org/10.1080/0158791042000262139

Salthouse, T. A. (1992). Why do adult age differences increase with task complexity? *Developmental Psychology, 28*(5), 905.

Sanchez, I., & Gunawardena, C. N. (1998). Understanding and supporting the culturally diverse distance learner. In C. C. Gibson (Ed.), *Distance learners in higher education: institutional responses for quality outcomes* (pp. 47–64). Atwood.

Savidge, N. (2017, October 12). University of Wisconsin officials announce plan to merge Colleges with four-year campuses. *Wisconsin State Journal.* http://host.madison.com/wsj/news/local/education/university/university-of-wisconsin-officials-announce-plan-to-merge-colleges-with/article_ad06107e-58a7-5ede-9565-0a7b91e08242.html

Schimke, D., Stoeger, H., & Ziegler, A. (2007). The relationship between social presence and group identification within online communities and its impact on the success of online communities. *Lecture Notes in Computer Science, 4564,* 160–168. https://doi.org/10.1007/978-3-540-73257-0_18

Schoenfeld, R., Lehmann, W., & Leplow, B. (2010). Effects of age and sex in mental rotation and spatial learning from virtual environments. *Journal of Individual Differences, 31*(2), 78–82. https://doi.org/10.1027/1614-0001/a000014

Schuler, D., & Namioka, A. (Eds.). (1993). *Participatory design: Principles and practices.* CRC.

Seaman, J. E., Allen, I. E., & Seaman, J. (2018). *Grade increase: Tracking distance education in the United States.* Babson Survey Research Group.

Shearer, R. L., Gregg, A., & Joo, K. P. (2015). Deep learning in distance education: Are we achieving the goal? *American Journal of Distance Education, 29*(2), 126–134. https://doi.org/10.1080/08923647.2015.1023637

Shute, V. J., & Kim, Y. J. (2014). Formative and stealth assessment. In D. Jonassen (Ed.), *Handbook of research on educational communications and technology* (pp. 311–321). Springer.

Simon, C. (2016). *Impossible to ignore: Creating memorable content to influence decisions.* McGraw Hill.

Smith, D. R., & Ayers, D. F. (2006). Culturally responsive pedagogy and online learning: Implications for the globalized community college. *Community College Journal of Research and Practice, 30*(5–6), 401–415. https://doi.org/10.1080/10668920500442125

Snyder, T. D., & Dillow, S. A. (2011). *Digest of Education Statistics, 2010* (NCES 2011-015). National Center for Education Statistics.

Soegaard, M. (2018). *The basics of user experience design.* Interaction Design Foundation.

Song, L., & Hill, J. R. (2007). A conceptual model for understanding self-directed learning in online environments. *Journal of Interactive Online Learning, 6*(1), 27–42.

Stone, N. J. (2000). Exploring the relationship between calibration and self-regulated learning. *Educational Psychology Review, 12*(4), 437–475. https://doi.org/10.1023/A:1009084430926

Sung, E., & Mayer, R. E. (2012). Five facets of social presence in online distance education. *Computers in Human Behavior, 28,* 1738–1747. https://doi.org/10.1016/j.chb.2012.04.014

Swan, K., Bowman, J., Holmes, A., Schweig, S., & Vargas, J. (1998). "Reading" the web: Making sense on the information superhighway. *Journal of Educational Technology Systems, 27*(2), 95–104. https://doi.org/10.2190/7Y4Q-XTU1-1MG1-MH1N

Swan, K., Shea, P., Fredericksen, E., Pickett, A., Pelz, W., & Maher, G. (2000). Building knowledge building communities: Consistency, contact and communication in the virtual classroom. *Journal of Educational Computing Research, 23*(4), 359–383. https://doi.org/10.2190/W4G6-HY52-57P1-PPNE

Sweller, J. (1994). Cognitive load theory, learning difficulty, and instructional design. *Learning and Instruction, 4*(4), 295–312. https://doi.org/10.1016/0959-4752(94)90003-5

Sweller, J., Ayres, P. L., Kalyuga, S., & Chandler, P. A. (2003). The expertise reversal effect. *Educational Psychologist, 38*(1), 23–31. https://doi.org/10.1207/S15326985EP3801_4

Tractinsky, N., Katz, A. S., & Ikar, D. (2000). What is beautiful is usable. *Interacting with computers, 13*(2), 127–145. https://doi.org/10.1016/S0953-5438(00)00031-X

Tuch, A. N., Roth, S. P., Hornbæk, K., Opwis, K., & Bargas-Avila, J. A. (2012). Is beautiful really usable? Toward understanding the relation between usability, aesthetics, and affect in HCI. *Computers in Human Behavior, 28*(5), 1596–1607. https://doi.org/10.1016/j.chb.2012.03.024

Twenge, J. M. (2014). *Generation me—Revised and updated: Why today's young Americans are more confident, assertive, entitled—and more miserable than ever before.* Free Press.

Tyng, C. M., Amin, H. U., Saad, M. N. M., & Malik, A. S. (2017). The influences of emotion on learning and memory. *Frontiers in Psychology, 8,* 1454. http://doi.org/10.3389/fpsyg.2017.01454

Ubell, R. (2016, December 13). *Why faculty still don't want to teach online.* https://www.insidehighered.com/advice/2016/12/13/advice-faculty-members-about-overcoming-resistance-teaching-online-essay

University of Wisconsin System. (2018). *UW flex option.* https://flex.wisconsin.edu/

van Merriënboer, J. G., & Kirschner, P. A. (2018). *Ten steps to complex learning: A systematic approach to four-component instructional design.* Routledge.

Vansteenkiste, M., Lens, W., & Deci, E. L. (2006). Intrinsic versus extrinsic goal contents in self-determination theory: Another look at the quality of academic motivation. *Educational Psychologist, 41*(1), 19–31. https://doi.org/10.1207/s15326985ep4101_4

Walker, C. E., & Kelly, E. (2007). Online instruction: Student satisfaction, kudos, and pet peeves. *Quarterly Review of Distance Education, 8*(4), 309–319.

Wei, C. W., & Chen, N. S. (2012). A model for social presence in online classrooms. *Educational Technology Research and Development, 60*(3), 529–545. https://doi.org/10.1007/s11423-012-9234-9

Wei, C. W., Hung, I. C., Lee, L., & Chen, N. S. (2011). A joyful classroom learning system with robot learning companion for children to learn mathematics multiplication. *The Turkish Online Journal of Education Technology, 10*(2), 11–23.

Weise, M. R., & Christensen, C. M. (2014). *Hire education: Mastery, modularization, and the workforce revolution.* Clayton Christensen Institute for Disruptive Innovation.

Welsh, M. A., & Dehler, G. E. (2012). Combining critical reflection and design thinking to develop integrative learners. *Journal of Management Education, 37*(6), 771–802. https://doi.org/10.1177/1052562912470107

Wiggins, G., Wiggins, G. P., & McTighe, J. (2005). *Understanding by design.* ASCD.

Williams, R. G. (1977). A behavioral typology of educational objectives for the cognitive domain. *Educational Technology, 17*(6), 39–46. http://doi.org/10.2307/44421172

Wittwer, J., & Renkl, A. (2008). Why instructional explanations often do not work: A framework for understanding the effectiveness of instructional explanations. *Educational Psychologist, 43*(1), 49–64. https://doi.org/10.1080/004615 20701756420

Wolfson, N. E., Cavanagh, T. M., & Kraiger, K. (2014). Older adults and technology-based instruction: Optimizing learning outcomes and transfer. *Academy of Management Learning & Education, 13*(1), 26–44. https://doi.org/10.5465/ amle.2012.0056

Xu, D., & Jaggars, S. (2013). *Adaptability to online learning: Differences across types of students and academic subject areas.* Community College Research Center, Columbia University.

Zhang, Q., & Oetzel, J. G. (2006). Constructing and validating a teacher immediacy scale: A Chinese perspective. *Communication Education, 55*(2), 218–241. https://doi.org/10.1080/03634520600566231

Zimmerman, B., & Martinez-Pons, M. (1988, September). Construct validation of a strategy model of student self-regulated learning. *Journal of Educational Psychology, 80*, 284–290. https://doi.org/10.1037/0022-0663.80.3.284

Zull, J. E. (2002). *The art of changing the brain: Enriching teaching by exploring the biology of learning.* Stylus.

ABOUT THE AUTHORS

Simone C.O. Conceição has over 25 years of professional experience in distance teaching and learning and training. She holds an MA in adult and continuing education leadership from the University of Wisconsin-Milwaukee and a PhD in adult learning and distance education from the University of Wisconsin–Madison. She is a professor and chair in the Department of Administrative Leadership at the University of Wisconsin-Milwaukee. Online education, adult learning, impact of technology on teaching and learning, learning design, and staff development and training have been part of the core themes throughout her numerous peer-reviewed publications and coauthorship/editorship of 10 books. Her work and publications focus on online presence, learning design, and faculty workload, among other topics. She has served on the editorial board of several journals focusing on adult, continuing, and online education and is editor-in-chief of *eLearn Magazine*. She has been invited to give talks, provide professional development, and collaborate with others in Chile, Dominican Republic, Brazil, Turkey, and China. Her professional network, experience, and leadership provide a unique perspective for the fields of adult and continuing education, educational technology, and online education in a time challenged by societal, technological, and global changes. She has received two career awards, two alumni awards, and one research award. In 2018, she was inducted into the International Adult and Continuing Education Hall of Fame.

Les L. Howles has over 30 years professional experience in distance education, eLearning, media production, and instructional design. He has held multiple positions at the University of Wisconsin-Madison including director of distance education professional development, team leader for the Learning Solutions group and senior eLearning consultant. Throughout his career, Howles has developed and taught online courses, designed educational software, and led groups of professionals in creating innovative learning solutions for education and training. He has worked in multiple industries including higher education, corporate training, government, health care, K–12 and is an independent learning design strategist for Howles Associates. He serves on the editorial board of *eLearn Magazine* and has authored and coauthored

numerous articles for professional publications. Howles holds undergradu-
ate degrees from Saint Edward's University and the State University of New
York. He earned his graduate degree in educational technology from the
University of Oregon. Howles has been a frequent presenter at regional,
national, and international conferences and directed the annual Distance
Teaching & Learning Conference in Madison, Wisconsin.

absorb-type activities, 86–87
academic performance, 20
active learning strategies, 67, 153
ADDIE. *See* analysis, design,
    development, implementation,
    and evaluation
aesthetics, 153
  of course interface, 35, 49, 58, 59
  of emotional dimension, 27
  of online learning environment,
    52
age differences (learner
    characteristics), 16, 20–21, 153
Allen, M. W., 79, 88
analysis, design, development,
    implementation, and
    evaluation (ADDIE), 88
aptitude (learner characteristics), 16,
    21–22, 153
ARCS. *See* attention, relevance,
    confidence, and satisfaction
assessments and feedback (design
    aspect), xiv, 34, 35, 36, 153
  asynchronous discussion in,
    129–30
  behavioral design principle in,
    127, 130
  cognitive elements in, 128–30
  concept mapping in, 128–29
  in course design aspects, 32–33
  curiosity in, 128–30
  deep learning embedding
    through, 130

design strategies for, 149–50
emotional elements in, 128–30
gamification in, 132
instructor feedback in, 124–25
of integrated framework for
    designing the online learning
    experience, 24
learner agency integration in, 127
learner creation of, 132–33
learner feedback through, on
    course design, 133
with learner growth mindset, 128
learner motivation in, 125–27,
    132–33
learner self-assessment in, 124
as learning experience, 123–27,
    130–33
learning experience design
    incorporating, 121–22,
    127–34
new approaches in, 134–35
problem-based learning in, 131
quizzes in, 130–31
scenario-based activities in, 131
spacing and interleaving, 123–24,
    159
asynchronous online group, 118,
    129–30
asynchronous social interactions,
    105–6, 108, 109
atomistic learning design, 86
attention, relevance, confidence, and
    satisfaction (ARCS), 77–78

Baker, C., 30
Baruth, O., 19–20
behavioral design principle, 153
  in assessments and feedback, 127,
    130
  in learning experience design, 35
behavioral dimension, 153
  of integrated framework for
    designing the online learning
    experience, 24, 28–29
  learner interaction with
    technology in, 29
  of learning experience design, 7–8
behavioral engagement, 115–16
being, 30
beliefs and values, 116
Bloom, B., 24
Boud, D., 122
brainstorming
  in design thinking, 12
  in French and Italian literature
    course design, 92–93
Broadbent, J., 18
broad-brush to targeted content,
    70–71
Brockett, R. G., 18
Burkman, E, 73

calibration, 19, 125
Campbell, P., 27
Candy, P. C., 18
Chang, S. C., 51
Cho, V., 51
Clark, R. E., 66
Cleveland-Innes, M, 27
Coates, H., 43
cognitive capacity, 21
  in cognitive dimension, 25–26
cognitive design principle, 34, 153
cognitive dimension, 48, 153

cognitive capacity in, 25–26
  deep learning in, 25
  of integrated framework for
    designing the online learning
    experience, 24–26
  of learning experience design, 7
  of pedagogical wrappers, 101
cognitive dominance, 73–74
cognitive elements, 128–30
cognitive engagement, 34, 115–16
cognitive load
  in French and Italian literature
    course, 90
  management of, 26, 34
Cohen, A., 19–20
communication style, 35,
    115. See also personalized
    communication
Conceição, S. C. O., 30, 125–26
concept map, 153
  in assessments and feedback,
    128–29
  as learner-centered activity, 129
conceptual model, 154
  of course structure and interface,
    40–41, 52–53
  definition of, 40
  of learner interface, 45
  of LMS, 43
confidence, in emotional design,
    77–78
connect-type activities, 86–87
consumer finance, 47–48
content design, 66. See also
    instructional content design
  and social discourse, 35
content formatting, 45–46
content interactions (design aspect),
    154. See also learner-content
    interactions

in course design aspects, 32, 33,
        147–48
    of integrated framework for
        designing the online learning
        experience, 24
content type, in instructional
        content design, 65, 66–67
contextualization, 33
    in learner-content interactions,
        72, 79–82
copresence, 36, 154
course climate facilitation
    pedagogical wrappers in, 113–14
    in social interactions, 112–14
course design aspects, xiii, 154.
        See also French and Italian
        literature course design
    assessments and feedback in,
        32–33
    content interactions in, 32, 33,
        147–48
    course structure and interface of,
        31–32
    of integrated framework for
        designing the online learning
        experience, 31–33
course interface, 35, 49, 58, 59
course structure and interface
        (design aspect), 39, 154
    conceptual models of, 40–41,
        52–53
    core topics and tasks, 53–54
    of course design aspects, 31–32
    design challenges of, 42–45
    design content elements for
        understandability in, 57–58
    design of learner interface in,
        55–59
    design strategies for, 147
    feedback on, 54, 56–57

functional prototypes for, 58–59
    information architecture of,
        55–56
    of integrated framework for
        designing the online learning
        experience, 24
    learner interface in, 45–52, 55–59
    LMS influencing, 31
    organization in, 53–55
    strategies for, 52–59
critical reading, 89, 95
culture and ethnicity (learner
        characteristics), 16, 21, 154
curation, in online content design
        factors, 63–64
curiosity, 78–79, 97
    in assessments and feedback,
        128–30

decontextualized to contextualized
        content, 71–72
deep learning, 34, 154
    assessments and feedback
        embedded in, 130
    in cognitive dimension, 25
    social engagement through, 36,
        116–18
    social interactions through,
        116–18
Dennen, V. P., 30
design
    of online learning experience,
        146–52
    of pedagogical wrappers, 75
design challenges
    of course structure and interface,
        42–45
    in design thinking, 12
    face-to-face to online conversion,
        43–44

for French and Italian literature
course, 90–92
design content elements, 57–58
design factors, 51–52
of social interactions, 106–12
design questions and strategies, 146,
147–51
design research, 5
design solutions, 12
design strategies
for assessments and feedback,
149–50
for social interactions, 149
design task development, 110
design thinking, xiv, 40, 154. *See
also* learning experience design
definition of, 10
empathic design in, 11, 96–98
implementation in, 12, 146
key practices of, 11–12
learner empathy in, 11–12
for learning experience creation,
137–46
in learning experience design,
10–12
for online design strategies, with
empathic mindset, 96–98
phases and steps for, 97
dialogue, with learner, 122
didactic strategies, 67, 154
digital learning ecosystem, 146
in learning experience design,
42–43
digital pedagogies, 44
in learner-content interactions,
63, 64, 76
learning experience design in,
6–7
science microlearning module in,
76

dimensions of learning, 23, 36–37,
154
discipline-specific content
interactions, 62
distant education, xi
D'Mello, S., 25, 26
domain knowledge, 42
domain-specific knowledge, 44
do-type activities, 86–87

emotional and behavioral interplay,
73–74
emotional connections, 114–15
emotional design, 155
ARCS of, 77–78
attention, relevance, confidence,
and satisfaction in, 77–78
in learner-content interactions,
77–79
emotional design principle, 155
in learning experience design, 9,
34–35
emotional dimension, 155
of integrated framework for
designing the online learning
experience, 24, 26–28
of learning experience design,
7–8
of pedagogical wrappers, 101
emotional elements, 128–30
emotional presence, 27–28, 155
empathic design, xv, 155
in design thinking, 11–12, 96–98
four Cs of, 96–98
end-of-course debriefing, 119
enrollments, 1–2
ethnicity. *See* culture and ethnicity
(learner characteristics)
expert reversal effect, 66
explanatory presentations, 155

extrinsic motivation, 17

face-to-face, to online conversion, 43–44
facilitated communication, 115
feedback, 122, 144. *See also*
  assessments and feedback
  of course structure and interface, 54, 56–57
  five types of, 125–26
  for French and Italian literature course design, 90–92
  learner empathy in, 126
  with screencasting, 126–27
  from students, 89, 91
  with text, 126
  with voice, 126–27
feedback, from learners, 142, 144
female learners, 22–23
Fink, L. D., 86–87, 123
flow, 155
flow and engagement, 123–24
Foreman, S., 4
formative assessment, 155
four Cs of empathic design, 11–12, 96–98, 155
four learning dimensions, 37
fragmentation, 69–70
  in atomistic learning design, 86
  in course structure and interface, 55
  in French and Italian literature course design, 90
  to integration, 69–70
French and Italian literature course design
  critical reading in, 89, 95
  design challenge definition in, 90–92
  feedback for, 90–92

implementation in, 95–97
interactive hypermedia document of, 95, 97
learner empathy in, 89–90
in learning experience design, 88–97
pedagogical wrappers in, 95–96
prototype design ideas in, 93–94
real-world context design in, 94–95
functional fixedness, 11

gamification, 132, 155
Garrett, J. J., 5
Garrison, D. R., 18, 31
gender differences (learner characteristics), 16, 22–23, 156
goal, 18, 40–41
  of course structure and interface, 52–53
Graesser, A., 25, 26
group discussion, 111
  asynchronous, 129–30
  in French and Italian literature course design, 95
  for pedagogical wrappers, 112
group responsibility, 113
growth mindset, 128, 156

HCI. *See* human-computer interactions
Hiemstra, R., 18
higher education, 1–2
holistic design, 86
Horn, R. E., 48, 58
Horton, W., 79–80, 86–87
human-centered design, 5
human-computer interactions (HCI), 27, 46
human-computer systems, 9–10

human factors design, 5
human support, 65, 68–69

idea prototypes, 12. *See also*
    prototype design ideas
identification, by name, 116
immediacy, 107
implementation, 37
    of design thinking, in learning
        experience design, 12, 146
inductive strategies, 67, 156
information architecture, 156
    of course structure and interface,
        55–56
    of learner interface, 46–48
    in online education, 46
information design, 156
    of learner interface, 48, 49
information overload, 21
innovative solutions, 2
    in learning experience design,
        140–41
instructional content design
    content type in, 65, 66–67
    curation of external content in,
        63–64
    discipline-specific content
        interactions in, 62
    instructional strategies of, 65, 67
    interaction design, content and,
        82–83
    learner characteristics of, 65, 66
    learner-content interactions shifts
        in, 69–74
    learner-content interactions
        strategies in, 71, 74–82
    learning objectives of, 65
    online content design factors in,
        64–74
    for online learning experience, 61
    process of, 61–64

situational factors in, 65, 68–69
story integration through, 80
technology affordances of, 65, 68
instructional strategies, 65, 67
instructor-facilitated discussion, 117
instructor feedback, 124–25
    learner self-assessment after, 134
instructor involvement, 114
instructor-learner interactions. *See*
    learner-instructor interactions
instructor scaffolding, 117
integrated framework for designing
    the online learning experience,
    xv, 103, 137, 156
    assessments and feedback of, 24
    behavioral dimension of, 24,
        28–29
    cognitive dimension of, 24–26
    course design aspects of, 31–33
    dimensions of, 23–31
    emotional dimension of, 24,
        26–28
    implementation of, 37
    learner characteristics in, 15–23
    learning activities of, 24
    learning design for, 10–12
    learning experience design in,
        33–37
    social dimension of, 24, 29–31
integration, 69–70, 127
integration design principle, 36–37
interaction design, 82–83
interactive case scenario, 83
interactive hypermedia document,
    95, 97
interactive text screenshot, 97
intertextuality, 89
interviews, 138, 139
intimacy, 107
intrinsic motivation, 17
introduction activity screenshot, 96

Janus, Professor, 88–90, 94–95, 98
Joo, Y. J., 51

Kahneman, D., 50
Keller, J., 73
Keller, J. M., 77–78
Kirschner, P. A., 53, 86
knowing-doing gap, 73–74
knowledge. *See* perception of
    self-knowledge (learner
    characteristics); prior
    knowledge (learner
    characteristics)
Kolb, A. Y., 6
Kolb, D. A., 6

Ladyshewsky, R., 30
Lavie, T., 52
learner agency, integration, 127
learner application, of knowledge,
    29
learner-centered activity, 129
learner-centered approach, 4, 55,
    101
learner-centered design, 8–9, 59,
    156
learner-centered interfaces, 56–57
learner-centered values, xii
learner characteristics, 34
    age differences as, 16, 20–21, 153
    aptitude as, 16, 21–22, 153
    culture and ethnicity as, 16, 21,
        154
    expert reversal effect as, 66
    gender differences as, 16, 22–23,
        156
    of instructional content design,
        65, 66
    in integrated framework for
        designing the online learning
        experience, 15–23

motivation as, 16, 17, 18, 22,
    157
perception of self-knowledge as,
    16, 19, 157
personality traits as, 16, 19–20,
    157
prior knowledge as, 16–17, 158
self-directedness as, 16, 18, 158
self-efficacy as, 16, 18–19, 158
self-regulation as, 16, 17–18, 158
social interactions affected by,
    108–9
learner-content interactions, xiii
    broad-brush to targeted content
        in, 70–71
    cognitive dominance to
        emotional behavioral interplay
        for, 73–74
    contextualization in, 71–72,
        79–82
    digital pedagogies in, 63, 64, 76
    emotional design in, 77–79
    fragmentation to integration of,
        69–70
    in instructional content design,
        69–82
    multimedia and instructional
        methods in, 76–77
    in online environment, 103
    pedagogical wrappers in, 74–75
    scenario narrative, context and,
        79, 81–82
    scenarios in, 79, 81–82
    shifts in, 69–74
    single media to hybridized media
        content for, 72–73
    stories in, 79–81
    strategies for, 70, 74–82
learner creation, 132–33
learner empathy. *See also* empathic
    design

in design thinking, 11–12
in feedback, 126
four Cs of, 11–12, 155
in French and Italian literature
  course design, 89–90
interviews for, 138
in learning experience design, 37,
  137–38
learner feedback, 133
learner growth mindset, 128
learner-instructor interactions, 30,
  103, 105, 106
learner interactions
  with other learners, 30–31
  with technology, xiii, 3, 29, 156
learner interface, xiii, 156
  conceptual model of, 45
  content formatting of, 45–46
  in course structure and interface,
    45–52, 55–59
  design factors influencing learner
    satisfaction in, 51–52
  of emotional connections,
    114–15
  information architecture of,
    46–48
  information design of, 48, 49
  structural framework of, 37
  visual design of, 35, 45–46,
    48–51
learner involvement
  asynchronous free-flow discussion
    in, 118
  end-of-course debriefing for, 119
  through social interactions,
    118–19
  virtual office hours for, 119
learner-learner interactions, 103,
  105
learner needs, 138–40
learner persona, 138

learner satisfaction, 51–52
learner self-assessment, 124, 133–34
learning, 7–8
learning activities (design aspect),
  xiii, 123, 157
  absorb-type activities as, 86–87
  connect-type activities as, 86–87
  in course design aspects, 32–33
  design strategies for, 88, 148
  do-type activities as, 86–87
  French and Italian literature
    course design in, 88–97
  of integrated framework for
    designing the online learning
    experience, 24
  in learning experience design,
    85–88
  online design strategies of, 88,
    96–101
  for the online environment, 87
  online types of, 86–87
learning context (self-monitoring),
  18
learning design
  dynamic learning ecosystem for,
    3–5
  integrated framework for
    designing the online learning
    experience, 10–12
  learner-centered approach in, 4
  learner experience design for,
    6–10
  mindset shift in, 3–4
  online, 4–5
  from other disciplines, 5
  tipping point in higher education
    with, 1–2
learning dimensions, 23, 36–37,
  154
learning ecosystem
  design of online, 4–5

learner-centered approach in, 4
for learning design, 3–5
LMS in, 68
mindset shift in, 3–4
from other disciplines, 5
social networking in, 3
technology in, 3, 4–5, 45
learning experience
assessments and feedback as,
121–27, 130–33
definition of, 6
design thinking creation for,
137–46
learning experience design, 157
assessments and feedback in,
121–22, 127–34
behavioral design principle in, 35
behavioral dimension of, 7–8
cognitive design principle in, 34
cognitive dimension of, 7
concepts for, 8–10
course focuses of, 42
definition of, 7–8, 15
design thinking in, 10–12
digital learning ecosystem in,
42–43
in digital pedagogies, 6–7
elements of, 34
emotional design principle in, 9,
34–35
emotional dimension of, 7–8
factors influencing, 142–43
feedback, from learners in, 142
French and Italian literature
course in, 88–97
innovative solutions in, 140–41
in integrated framework for
designing the online learning
experience, 33–37
integration design principle in,
36–37

learner-centered design in, 8–9
learner empathy in, 37, 137–38
learner needs in, 138–40
learner persona in, 138
learning activities in, 85–88
learning dimensions of, 36–37
online design strategies of,
96–101
participatory design in, 9–10
principles and strategies of,
33–37
problem statements in, 139–40
prototype design ideas in,
141–44
scenario-based activities in, 142
social design principle in, 36
social dimension of, 7–8
for social interactions, 110–19
supplements of, xii
synthesis of interviews in, 138
test in, 144–46
learning experience design
principles, 157
learning management system
(LMS), 4, 6, 64
conceptual model of, 43
course structure and interface
influenced by, 31
in learning ecosystem, 68
in online education, 26
surface layer of, 59
technology in, 40, 57
tools and templates of, 55
learning objectives (self-
management), 18, 35, 65,
107
learning solutions, 87–88
learning space, 51
learning task, 157
Lee, J., 123
Lehman, R. M., 30, 125–26

LMS. *See* learning management system
Loderer, K., 27
logistical communication, 115
long-term memory, 25
look and feel, 157

main menu, 47–48
male learners, 22–23
management systems, 43. *See also* learning management system
Mayer, R. E., 25, 28
McCracken, J., 123
media formats, 34
    hybrid multimedia, 76–77
    single to hybridized, 72–73
Medina, J., 70
metacognitive strategies, 17
microlearning. *See* science microlearning module
millennials, 2, 20
Miller, M. D., 28
mindset shift, 3–4
Molloy, E. K., 122
motivation (learner characteristics), 16, 18, 22, 157
    assessments and feedback in, 125–27, 132–33
    of deep learning, 34
    of emotional dimension, 28
    extrinsic, 17
    intrinsic, 17
    social interactions influence in, 108
    technology impacting, 126
multimedia and instructional methods, 76–77
multimedia software, 92–93
multiple learning task, 99–100

navigation, and wayfinding, 57
nontraditional students, 2
Norman, D., 5, 27, 45

OER. *See* open educational resources
online communication, 108
online content design factors, 63–74
online course
    behavioral engagement in, 115–16
    changing existing, 44–45
    cognitive dimension of, 48
    cognitive engagement in, 115–16
    domain knowledge in, 42
    holistic design of, 86
    main menu for, 47–48
    social interactions in, 111
online design strategies
    design thinking with empathic mindset for, 96–98
    learner-centered approach in, 101
    of learning activities (design aspect), 88, 96–101
    of learning experience design, 96–101
    multiple learning task inclusion in, 99–100
    pedagogical wrappers in, 100–101
    technology affordances in, 98–99
online education
    contextualization in, 33
    engagement in, 44
    enrollment growth in, 1–2
    information architecture in, 46
    LMS in, 26
online environment
    information architecture in, 46

learner-content interactions in, 103

learner-instructor interactions in, 103, 105, 106

learner-learner interactions in, 103, 105

learning activities for, 87

social interactions in, 103

online instructional contexts, 81–82

online learning environment, 52

online learning experience, 61, 146–52. *See also* integrated framework for designing the online learning experience

open educational resources (OER), 62, 64, 70

Orlando, J., 126

paralanguage, 108

participatory design, 9–10, 11, 157

pedagogical wrappers, 36, 128, 142, 157

cognitive dimension of, 101

in course climate facilitation, 113–14

design of, 75

emotional dimension of, 101

in French and Italian literature course design, 95–96

in learner-content interactions, 74–75

in online design strategies, 100–101

for social interactions, 112

perception of self-knowledge (learner characteristics), 16, 19, 157

personality model, 19

personality traits (learner characteristics), 16, 19–20, 157

personalized communication, 115–16, 158

personal responsibility orientation (goal and process), 18

Pfeffer, J., 73

photos and graphics, 116

Poon, W. L., 18

prior knowledge (learner characteristics), 16–17, 158

problem-based learning, 131, 158

problem statements, 139–40

procrastination, 19

prototype design ideas, 12

in French and Italian literature course design, 93–94

in learning experience design, 141–44

prototype design screenshot, 94

psychological factors, 4

quizzes, 130–31

rapid prototyping, xv

real world applications, xiv

real-world context design, 81, 94–95

relevance, 77–78

Renkl, A., 71

resources

investment, 65, 69

open educational, 62, 64, 70

return on investment factor (ROI), 69, 71

Rosenberg, M. J., 4

SAM. *See* successive approximation method

satisfaction

in emotional design, 77–78

learner, 51–52

of social interactions, 104–5
scaffolding. *See* instructor
  scaffolding
scenario-based activities, 131, 142,
  158
scenario-based learning activity,
  98–99
scenario narratives, 81–82
scenarios, 79, 81–82, 83
schemas, 16, 21, 66
science microlearning module, 76
screencasting, 126–27
screenshot
  interactive text, 97
  introduction activity, 96
  prototype design, 94
self-assessment. *See* learner
  self-assessment
self-directedness (learner
  characteristics), 16, 18, 158
self-efficacy (learner characteristics),
  16, 18–19, 158
self-regulation (learner
  characteristics), 16, 18, 158
  encouragement through learner
    self-assessment, 133–34
  as metacognitive strategies, 17
seven Cs framework, 81–82, 98,
  158
shallow learning, 25, 158
single media, to hybridized media
  content, 72–73
situational factors
  human aspects of, 65, 68–69
  in instructional content design,
    65, 68–69
  resource investment of, 65, 69
  technical aspects of, 65, 68
social climate, 36
social design principle, 36, 158

social dimension, 159
  of integrated framework for
    designing the online learning
    experience, 24, 29–31
  of learner interactions with
    instructor, 30
  of learner interactions with other
    learners, 30–31
  of learning experience design,
    7–8
social engagement
  through deep learning, 36,
    116–18
  discussion guidelines in, 117–18
  instructor-facilitated discussion
    in, 117
social interactions (design aspect),
    xiii–xiv, 159
  asynchronous, 105–6, 108, 109
  course climate facilitation in,
    112–14
  in course design aspects, 32–33
  through deep learning, 116–18
  design factors for, 106–12
  design strategies for, 149
  design task development for, 110
  emotional connections in,
    114–15
  formal *versus* informal, 105–6
  of integrated framework for
    designing the online learning
    experience, 24
  interpersonal communication via
    technology in, 103, 108
  intimacy and immediacy
    affecting, 107
  learner characteristics affecting,
    108–9
  learner involvement through,
    118–19

learning experience design for, 110–19
learning objectives in, 107
motivation influences in, 108
in online course, 111
in online environment, 103
pedagogical wrappers for, 112
personalized communication in, 115–16
satisfaction of, 104–5
as synchronous, 105–6, 108, 109
types of, 105–6
social networking, 3
spacing, and interleaving assessments, 123–24, 159
stories, 142, 159
in course climate facilitation, 113
interweaving, throughout lesson, 80–81
in learner-content interactions, 79–81
structural framework
alternatives to, 54
content scope of, 41
of course content units, 45
of information architecture, 55
of learner interface, 37
templates for, 43
thematic units of, 41–42
student demographics, 1–2
successive approximation method (SAM), 88
summative assessment, 159
surface layer, 59
Sutton, R. I., 73
Swan, K., 45
synchronous social interactions, 105–6, 108, 109
synthesis, of feedback from students class discussions in, 89, 91

lecture presentation in, 89, 91
reading assignments in, 89, 91
synthesis, of interviews, 138
task
completion, 133–34
design, development, 110
learning, 157
multiple learning, 99–100
technology
in age differences, 20
behavioral dimension in, 29
learner interaction with, xiii, 3, 156
in learning ecosystem, 3, 4–5, 45
in LMS, 40, 57
motivation impacted by, 126
in social interactions, 103
social interactions shaped by, 108
technology affordances
of instructional content design, 65, 68
in learning solutions, 87–88
of multimedia software, 92–93
in online design strategies, 98–99
in scenario-based learning activity, 98–99
test, 12, 144–46
tools, and templates, 55
Tractinsky, N., 52
Tung, F. C., 51

user experience design (UXD)
concepts and principles of, 39
key concepts of, 6
Norman establishment of, 5
strategies from, 55
user interface in, 46
user interface, 46
UXD. *See* user experience design

van Merriënboer, J. G., 53, 86
virtual cafe, 113
virtual office hours, 119, 133
virtual team project, 129
visual content, 49
visual design, 35, 45–46, 48–51

voice, 126–27

wireframes, 56–57
Wittwer, J., 71
working memory, 25

Also available from Stylus

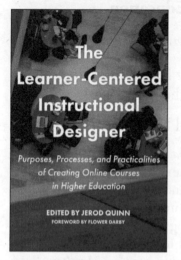

The Learner-Centered Instructional Designer

Purpose, Process, and Practicalities of Creating Online Courses in Higher Education

Edited by Jerod Quinn

This is a practical handbook for established and aspiring instructional designers in higher education, readers who may also be identified by such professional titles as educational developer, instructional technologist, or online learning specialist.

Jerod Quinn, together with a team of experienced instructional designers who have worked extensively with a wide range of faculty on a multiplicity of online courses across all types of institutions, offer key guiding principles, insights, and advice on how to develop productive and collegial partnerships with faculty to deliver courses that engage students and promote enduring learning.

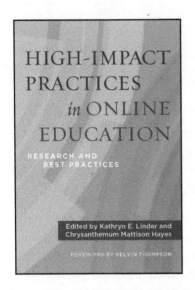

High-Impact Practices in Online Education

Research and Best Practices

Edited by Kathryn E. Linder and Chrysanthemum Mattison Hayes

Foreword by Kelvin Thompson

"*High-Impact Practices in Online Education* asks the right questions about online teaching and learning. This collection offers grounded, practical suggestions for evolving online pedagogy toward a purposeful form of teaching that offers possibilities beyond anything we've done until now."—*Matthew Reed, Vice President for Learning, Brookdale Community College*

"This timely and much-needed publication clearly shows that it is possible to engage learners in high-impact practices online. The book opens an entirely new realm of possibilities in which instructors and learners can confidently delve into the digital world in a way that provides purpose, equity in learning, and success."—*Susana Rivera-Mills, Provost and Executive Vice President for Academic Affairs, Ball State University*

99 Tips for Creating Simple and Sustainable Educational Videos

A Guide for Online Teachers and Flipped Classes

Karen Costa

Foreword by Michelle Pacansky-Brock

"Reading *99 Tips for Creating Simple and Sustainable Educational Videos* is like sitting down with an old friend and learning all of her best strategies for producing video content that will both help and motivate students in their learning. I loved the simplicity and practicality of Costa's suggestions and think that this is the perfect book for instructors who want to dip their toes in the video production waters but are not sure where to start."—***Kathryn E. Linder***, *Executive Director of Program Development, Kansas State University Global Campus*

The research is clear: Online learning works best when faculty build regular, positive, and interactive relationships with students. A strategy that helps forge such a relationship is the use of videos. Student satisfaction and course engagement levels also increase with the use of instructor-generated videos—the subject of this book.

Beginning by outlining the different types of videos you can create, and what the research says about their effectiveness, Karen Costa explains how they can be designed to reinforce learning, to align with and promote course outcomes, and to save you time across your courses. She then describes how to create successful videos with commonly available technologies such as your smartphone, and without a major investment of time, demonstrating the simple steps she took to develop her bank of videos and build her confidence to deliver short, straightforward learning aids that are effective and personal.

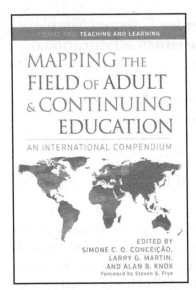

Mapping the Field of Adult and Continuing Education

An International Compendium
Volume 2: Teaching and Learning

Edited by Simone C. O. Conceição, Larry G. Martin, and Alan B. Knox

Foreword by Steven B. Frye

The field of adult and continuing education (ACE) has long been influential beyond its already porous borders and continues to be a source of important ideas, inspiration, and innovative practices for those in disciplines such as educational administration, social work, nursing, and counseling. Recognizing this, the American Association for Adult and Continuing Education (AAACE) commissioned the editors to create this compendium, which provides an invaluable resource to readers already established in the field, those entering the field, and to myriad neighbors of the field.

This four-volume compendium (also available as a combined ebook) brings together a host of national and international contributors to map the field of ACE in a series of brief articles addressing key theories and practices across its many domains and settings.

Volume two addresses teaching and learning topics ranging from methods and roles to programs and materials. This volume encompasses formal and informal learning as well as the variety of focus and setting, from cultural to occupational, and explores the wide range of theory and practice in ACE.

22883 Quicksilver Drive
Sterling, VA 20166-2019   Subscribe to our e-mail alerts: www.Styluspub.com